O'REILLY®

Strata
Making Data Work

Learn how to turn data into decisions.

From startups to the Fortune 500, smart companies are betting on data-driven insight, seizing the opportunities that are emerging from the convergence of four powerful trends:

- New methods of collecting, managing, and analyzing data

- Cloud computing that offers inexpensive storage and flexible, on-demand computing power for massive data sets

- Visualization techniques that turn complex data into images that tell a compelling story

- Tools that make the power of data available to anyone

Get control over big data and turn it into insight with O'Reilly's Strata offerings. Find the inspiration and information to create new products or revive existing ones, understand customer behavior, and get the data edge.

O'REILLY®

Visit oreilly.com/data to learn more.

Writing and Querying MapReduce Views in CouchDB

Bradley Holt

O'REILLY®

Beijing · Cambridge · Farnham · Köln · Sebastopol · Tokyo

Writing and Querying MapReduce Views in CouchDB
by Bradley Holt

Published by O'Reilly Media, Inc., 1005 Gravenstein Highway North, Sebastopol, CA 95472.

O'Reilly books may be purchased for educational, business, or sales promotional use. Online editions are also available for most titles (*http://my.safaribooksonline.com*). For more information, contact our corporate/institutional sales department: (800) 998-9938 or *corporate@oreilly.com*.

Editor:	Mike Loukides	**Cover Designer:**	Karen Montgomery
Production Editor:	Adam Zaremba	**Interior Designer:**	David Futato
Proofreader:	Adam Zaremba	**Illustrator:**	Robert Romano

February 2011:   First Edition.

Revision History for the First Edition:
   2011-01-20   First release
   2011-10-19   Second release
See *http://oreilly.com/catalog/errata.csp?isbn=9781449303129* for release details.

ISBN: 978-1-449-30312-9

[LSI]

1319043534

Table of Contents

Preface

Conventions Used in This Book

The following typographical conventions are used in this book:

Italic
> Indicates new terms, URLs, email addresses, filenames, and file extensions.

`Constant width`
> Used for program listings, as well as within paragraphs to refer to program elements such as variable or function names, databases, data types, environment variables, statements, and keywords.

`Constant width bold`
> Shows commands or other text that should be typed literally by the user.

`Constant width italic`
> Shows text that should be replaced with user-supplied values or by values determined by context.

 This icon signifies a tip, suggestion, or general note.

 This icon indicates a warning or caution.

Using Code Examples

This book is here to help you get your job done. In general, you may use the code in this book in your programs and documentation. You do not need to contact us for permission unless you're reproducing a significant portion of the code. For example, writing a program that uses several chunks of code from this book does not require permission. Selling or distributing a CD-ROM of examples from O'Reilly books does require permission. Answering a question by citing this book and quoting example code does not require permission. Incorporating a significant amount of example code from this book into your product's documentation does require permission.

We appreciate, but do not require, attribution. An attribution usually includes the title, author, publisher, and ISBN. For example: "*Writing and Querying MapReduce Views in CouchDB* by Bradley Holt (O'Reilly). Copyright 2011 Bradley Holt, 978-1-449-30312-9."

If you feel your use of code examples falls outside fair use or the permission given above, feel free to contact us at *permissions@oreilly.com*.

Safari® Books Online

Safari Books Online is an on-demand digital library that lets you easily search over 7,500 technology and creative reference books and videos to find the answers you need quickly.

With a subscription, you can read any page and watch any video from our library online. Read books on your cell phone and mobile devices. Access new titles before they are available for print, and get exclusive access to manuscripts in development and post feedback for the authors. Copy and paste code samples, organize your favorites, download chapters, bookmark key sections, create notes, print out pages, and benefit from tons of other time-saving features.

O'Reilly Media has uploaded this book to the Safari Books Online service. To have full digital access to this book and others on similar topics from O'Reilly and other publishers, sign up for free at *http://my.safaribooksonline.com*.

How to Contact Us

Please address comments and questions concerning this book to the publisher:

O'Reilly Media, Inc.
1005 Gravenstein Highway North
Sebastopol, CA 95472
800-998-9938 (in the United States or Canada)
707-829-0515 (international or local)
707-829-0104 (fax)

We have a web page for this book, where we list errata, examples, and any additional information. You can access this page at:

http://www.oreilly.com/catalog/9781449303129

To comment or ask technical questions about this book, send email to:

bookquestions@oreilly.com

For more information about our books, courses, conferences, and news, see our website at *http://oreilly.com*.

Find us on Facebook: *http://facebook.com/oreilly*

Follow us on Twitter: *http://twitter.com/oreillymedia*

Watch us on YouTube: *http://www.youtube.com/oreillymedia*

Content Updates

October 19, 2011

- Added a new chapter, Chapter 5.
- Updated screenshots and cURL examples to use CouchDB 1.1.0.
- Addressed a few changes and new features in CouchDB 1.1.0.
- Updated some hyperlinks to referenced resources and technologies.

Acknowledgments

I'd first like to thank Damien Katz, creator of CouchDB, and all of CouchDB's contributors. The CouchDB community—via the #couchdb IRC channel on Freenode—was very helpful in entertaining my questions while writing this book. J. Chris Anderson and MC Brown of Couchbase (*http://www.couchbase.com/*) provided valuable feedback. Hadi Hariri provided the inspiration for the addition of Chapter 5, MapReduce Views for SQL Users, to the second edition of this book. Bill Karwin (SQL expert and author of *SQL Antipatterns: Avoiding the Pitfalls of Database Programming* (*http://prag prog.com/book/bksqla/sql-antipatterns*)) provided a *very* helpful technical review of Chapter 5, MapReduce Views for SQL Users. Mike Loukides, this book's editor, and the rest of the team at O'Reilly Media were very responsive and helpful. I'd also like to thank Jason Pelletier and Steve Parmer—my colleagues at Found Line—for helping to review the material in this book. Any errors or omissions that remain are of my own making, and not the fault of any of the aforementioned reviewers.

CHAPTER 1

Introduction

If you are reading this book, then you likely have already installed CouchDB, explored the *Futon* web administration console, and created a few documents using the *cURL* command-line tool. You may even have created a CouchApp or other type of application that accesses documents stored in a CouchDB database. However, to use CouchDB for any practical application, you will likely need to create *MapReduce* views that let you query your database for meaningful data.

> The examples in this book were created using CouchDB 1.1.0. Features and interfaces may change in future versions of CouchDB.

Resources for Installing CouchDB

This book assumes that you have already installed CouchDB and have it up and running. If you need help with installation and setup, you may want to reference *CouchDB: The Definitive Guide* (*http://oreilly.com/catalog/9780596155902/*) (O'Reilly), which has instructions for installing CouchDB on Unix-like systems, Mac OS X, and Windows, as well as instructions for installing from source. You can also find help on the Installation (*http://wiki.apache.org/couchdb/Installation*) page of the CouchDB Wiki.

> An easy way to get CouchDB up-and-running is to install Couchbase Single Server (*http://www.couchbase.com/products-and-services/couch base-single-server*), which is powered by CouchDB. Couchbase implements a superset of the CouchDB API, meaning that it works just like CouchDB. In addition to the core CouchDB features, Couchbase also comes with GeoCouch built-in. GeoCouch provides the ability to do geospatial indexing and querying. Couchbase offers both community and enterprise editions. Support options are available for the enterprise editions.

Futon

Like many other databases, CouchDB provides a graphical user interface from which to access and administer the database. In CouchDB, this tool is called Futon, a web administration console. Once CouchDB is installed and running, Futon can be accessed using your web browser at *http://localhost:5984/_utils/* (see Figure 1-1). You can use Futon to create, read, update, and delete databases and documents. While beyond the scope of this book, Futon can also be used to configure your CouchDB install, replicate between CouchDB databases, view the status of CouchDB tasks, run the CouchDB test suite, set up server admins, configure database security, and run compaction and cleanup maintenance tasks. Futon is very useful for learning how CouchDB works, but for most development work you will likely use CouchDB's *HTTP API* instead.

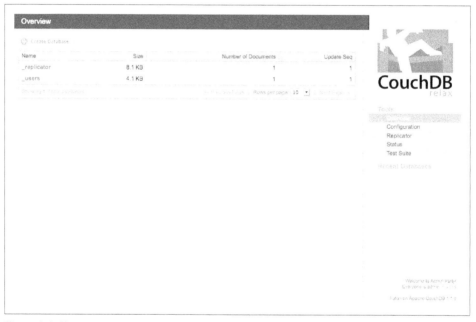

Figure 1-1. Futon

HTTP API

Developers interact with CouchDB using its RESTful HTTP API. Representational State Transfer (REST) is a software architecture style that describes distributed hyper-media systems such as the World Wide Web. In short, URIs are used to identify re-sources which can then be accessed using HTTP methods such as GET, POST, PUT, and DELETE. For example, with CouchDB you can POST a new document, GET a representation of an existing document, PUT an updated document, and DELETE a document. It is worth noting that REST is not limited to the Create, Read, Update, and Delete (CRUD) paradigm, yet this approach makes sense for CouchDB since it is a tool for persistent storage.

A truly RESTful system will also have hypermedia controls that inform a client of available state transitions. Fully RESTful applications can be built in CouchDB using list functions, show functions, and validation functions—all beyond the scope of this book. For more information, see the CouchDB Wiki pages on Formatting with Show and List (*http://wiki.apache.org/couchdb/Formatting_with_Show_and_List*) and Document Update Validation (*http://wiki.apache.org/couchdb/Document_Update_Validation*), or *CouchDB: The Definitive Guide* (*http://oreilly.com/catalog/9780596155902/*), Part 2: Developing with CouchDB. For more information on CouchDB's HTTP API, see the CouchDB Wiki pages on the HTTP Document API (*http://wiki.apache.org/couchdb/HTTP_Document_API*) and the HTTP View API (*http://wiki.apache.org/couchdb/HTTP_view_API*), or *CouchDB: The Definitive Guide* (*http://oreilly.com/catalog/9780596155902/*), Part 1: Introduction, Chapter 4: The Core API.

cURL

For those more comfortable with the command line than with a web interface, you can instead make HTTP requests directly to CouchDB using cURL. Use cURL's -X switch to specify the GET, POST, PUT, or DELETE HTTP method in your request to the specified URL (the default HTTP method is GET). Here is an example of using cURL to GET information about your CouchDB install (the GET HTTP method is specified for clarity even though it is the default):

```
curl -X GET http://localhost:5984/
```

The response:

```
{"couchdb":"Welcome","version":"1.1.0"}
```

Using cURL is a great way to familiarize yourself with CouchDB's HTTP API. Your application will make HTTP requests to CouchDB just like cURL does. You will likely not build an application using cURL since it could involve a lot of typing at the command line. Many platforms and programming languages have libraries that will make interacting with CouchDB easier. You can use either an HTTP client library or a library specifically designed to work with CouchDB. Using cURL gives you a glimpse into the features that these libraries will make available to you.

 Creating and updating design documents (covered in Chapter 3) using cURL can be difficult and time-consuming. There are several tools available that can help with this. The Python version of the CouchApp (*http://couchapp.org/*) command line tool is the most commonly used. There's also a Node.js version of the CouchApp command line tool called node.couchapp.js (*https://github.com/mikeal/node.couchapp.js*) and a Ruby command line tool called soca (*https://github.com/quirkey/soca*). Note that not all of these tools may be compatible with one another.

JSON

CouchDB stores documents as *JSON* (JavaScript Object Notation) objects. JSON is a human-readable and lightweight data interchange format. Data structures from many programming languages can easily be converted to and from JSON. The following is an example (that will be used in Chapter 2) of a JSON object representing a book:

```
{
    "_id":"978-0-596-15589-6",
    "title":"CouchDB: The Definitive Guide",
    "subtitle":"Time to Relax",
    "authors":[
        "J. Chris Anderson",
        "Jan Lehnardt",
        "Noah Slater"
    ],
    "publisher":"O'Reilly Media",
    "released":"2010-01-19",
    "pages":272
}
```

A JSON object is a collection of key/value pairs. The book object above contains the keys and values listed in Table 1-1. JSON values can be strings, numbers, booleans (false or true), arrays (e.g., ["J. Chris Anderson", "Jan Lehnardt", "Noah Slater"]), null, or another JSON object.

Table 1-1. Key/value pairs in a JSON book object

Key	Value
_id	A string representing the book's unique International Standard Book Number (ISBN)
title	A string representing the book's title
subtitle	A string representing the book's subtitle
authors	A JSON array of authors with each element being a string representing the author's name
publisher	A string representing the name of the publisher
released	A string representing the date in ISO 8601 format
pages	A number representing the number of pages contained within the book

CHAPTER 2

MapReduce

As the name suggests, MapReduce consists of a Map step and a Reduce step. Both the Map and Reduce steps can each be distributed in a way that takes advantage of the multiple processor cores that are found in modern hardware, allowing CouchDB to efficiently index your data. As documents are created, updated, and deleted, CouchDB is smart enough to run only modified documents through the Map step, reindexing only what has changed. The results of Reduce functions can often be cached as well.

We will use an example database named books in this chapter. To create this database using Futon (assuming CouchDB is installed on your local machine):

1. Navigate to *http://localhost:5984/_utils/* using your web browser.
2. Click "Create Database ...".
3. Enter **books** for the value of the "Database Name" field and click "Create" (see Figure 2-1).

Alternatively, you can create the books database using cURL:

```
curl -X PUT http://localhost:5984/books
```

The response:

```
{"ok":true}
```

Temporary Views

Map and Reduce are written as JavaScript functions that are defined within *views*. You can use a *temporary view* during development but should switch to using a view that is saved permanently for any real-world application. Temporary views can be very slow once you have more than a handful of documents. Views that are saved permanently are defined within *design documents*, which we'll talk about in Chapter 3.

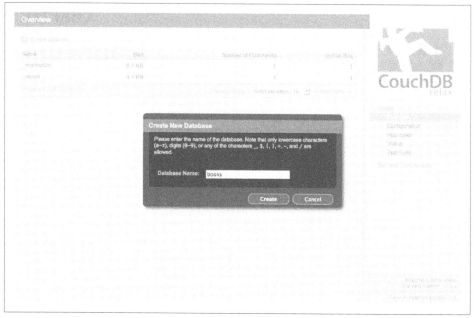

Figure 2-1. Creating a new database using Futon

Map

In the Map step, input documents are transformed, or mapped, from their original structure into a new key/value pair. For example, if your input document represents a book and contains information about the book's ISBN (the _id field in the following document), title, subtitle, authors, publisher, date released, and number of pages, then you may choose to map just the title. The result of this mapping for a single document would be the book's title. We'll use the following document representing a book in the examples in this chapter:

```
{
    "_id":"978-0-596-15589-6",
    "title":"CouchDB: The Definitive Guide",
    "subtitle":"Time to Relax",
    "authors":[
        "J. Chris Anderson",
        "Jan Lehnardt",
        "Noah Slater"
    ],
    "publisher":"O'Reilly Media",
    "released":"2010-01-19",
    "pages":272
}
```

Let's create this document in our books database now. Using Futon:

1. Navigate to *http://localhost:5984/_utils/* using your web browser and click on the books database that you created earlier.
2. From the "View" drop-down menu, select "All documents" if it is not already selected.
3. Click "New Document".
4. Click on the "Fields" tab if it is not already active.
5. Enter **978-0-596-15589-6** as the value of the _id field, and then click the "apply" ⊙ button.
6. Click on the "Source" tab.
7. Double-click on the source and paste in the contents of the above document, replacing the existing source, and then click the "apply" ⊙ button.
8. Click "Save Document".

Using cURL:

```
curl -X PUT http://localhost:5984/books/978-0-596-15589-6 -d \
"{
    \"_id\":\"978-0-596-15589-6\",
    \"title\":\"CouchDB: The Definitive Guide\",
    \"subtitle\":\"Time to Relax\",
    \"authors\":[
        \"J. Chris Anderson\",
        \"Jan Lehnardt\",
        \"Noah Slater\"
    ],
    \"publisher\":\"O'Reilly Media\",
    \"released\":\"2010-01-19\",
    \"pages\":272
}"
```

The response:

```
{"ok":true,"id":"978-0-596-15589-6","rev":"1-3a3fa1795fda0b9004849c3199f8b104"}
```

One-To-One Mapping

Assuming all of our book documents have exactly one `title` each, each document will Map to exactly one key/value pair. Here is a function that can Map the `title` field of our book documents:

```
function(doc) {
    if (doc.title) {
        emit(doc.title);
    }
}
```

Map | 7

Your Map function is passed one argument: a JSON object representing a document to be mapped. Your Map function will be called once for each document in your database. The call to the emit function is where the mapping happens. The emit function accepts two arguments: a key and a value. Both arguments are optional and will default to null if omitted. In the previous example, we make sure the document actually has a title before attempting to emit the title. Since it's helpful to know which document the mapped data came from, the id of the mapped document is also included automatically, as you'll see later.

 The key that is emitted is used when querying the data generated from your Map function. You can query a range of rows matching a starting and/or ending key, or rows matching a specific key. We'll explore how this is done in Chapter 4.

Let's create a temporary view using the above Map function:

1. Navigate to *http://localhost:5984/_utils/* using your web browser and click on the books database if you are not already there.
2. From the "View" drop-down menu, select "Temporary view...".
3. Paste the previous JavaScript function into the "Map Function" text box, replacing the existing function. Leave the "Reduce Function" text box empty.
4. Click the "Run" button (see Figure 2-2).

You can also create and query a temporary view using cURL:

```
curl -X POST http://localhost:5984/books/_temp_view \
-H "Content-Type: application/json" \
-d \
'{
    "map": "function(doc) {
        if (doc.title) {
            emit(doc.title);
        }
    }"
}'
```

The result from our temporary view (formatted for easier reading) is:

```
{
    "total_rows":1,
    "offset":0,
    "rows":[
        {
            "id":"978-0-596-15589-6",
            "key":"CouchDB: The Definitive Guide",
            "value":null
        }
    ]
}
```

Figure 2-2. Creating a temporary view of book titles using Futon

See Table 2-1 for the row in tabular format.

Table 2-1. Row from the titles temporary view

key	id	value
"CouchDB: The Definitive Guide"	"978-0-596-15589-6"	null

Mapping just one document isn't very interesting. Let's add a new document, representing a second book, using Futon in the same way you added the first book document:

```
{
    "_id":"978-0-596-52926-0",
    "title":"RESTful Web Services",
    "subtitle":"Web services for the real world",
    "authors":[
        "Leonard Richardson",
        "Sam Ruby"
    ],
    "publisher":"O'Reilly Media",
    "released":"2007-05-08",
    "pages":448
}
```

Map | 9

To add this document using cURL instead:

```
curl -X PUT http://localhost:5984/books/978-0-596-52926-0 -d \
"{
  \"_id\":\"978-0-596-52926-0\",
  \"title\":\"RESTful Web Services\",
  \"subtitle\":\"Web services for the real world\",
  \"authors\":[
    \"Leonard Richardson\",
    \"Sam Ruby\"
  ],
  \"publisher\":\"O'Reilly Media\",
  \"released\":\"2007-05-08\",
  \"pages\":448
}"
```

The response:

```
{"ok":true,"id":"978-0-596-52926-0","rev":"1-15e130dea4f192e26a6deb71974b7e51"}
```

Running our Map function again using Futon will now return both books, as shown in Figure 2-3.

Figure 2-3. Creating a temporary view of book titles using Futon, now with two book documents

Running our Map function again using cURL, we will also see both books returned:

```
{
    "total_rows":2,
    "offset":0,
    "rows":[
```

```
    {
        "id":"978-0-596-15589-6",
        "key":"CouchDB: The Definitive Guide",
        "value":null
    },
    {
        "id":"978-0-596-52926-0",
        "key":"RESTful Web Services",
        "value":null
    }
  ]
}
```

See Table 2-2 for the rows in tabular format.

Table 2-2. Rows from the titles temporary view with two books

key	id	value
"CouchDB: The Definitive Guide"	"978-0-596-15589-6"	null
"RESTful Web Services"	"978-0-596-52926-0"	null

 Rows in a view are collated by key first and then by document ID. String comparison in CouchDB is implemented according to the Unicode Collation Algorithm. You can switch the order of results in Futon by clicking the descending ▼ or ascending ▲ button next to the "Key" column label.

CouchDB also allows arbitrary JSON values as keys. This gives you a great amount of control over sorting and grouping rows. See the CouchDB documentation for details on the collation specification used by CouchDB.

One-To-Many Mapping

Let's now add a `formats` field to our two book documents. Each book can be available in `Print` format, in `Ebook` format, on `Safari Books Online`, or any combination of these three formats. This means that each document could map to multiple key/value pairs. If one book is available in `Print`, `Ebook`, and on `Safari Books Online`, then it will Map to three key/value pairs. If another book is available only in `Ebook` format and on `Safari Books Online`, it will Map to only two key/value pairs.

Let's add this new `formats` field to our two book documents. Both books are available in `Print`, `Ebook`, and on `Safari Books Online`. Using Futon:

1. Navigate to *http://localhost:5984/_utils/* using your web browser and click on the `books` database if you are not already there.

2. From the "View" drop-down menu, select "All documents" if it is not already selected.

Map | 11

3. Click on the second document listed (which was the first document we created): 978-0-596-15589-6.

4. Click "Add Field".

5. Enter **formats** as the field name, and then click the "apply" ◉ button.

6. Enter **["Print", "Ebook", "Safari Books Online"]** as the value, and then click the "apply" ◉ button. Figure 2-4 shows how everything should look.

7. Click "Save Document".

8. Return to the books database page and repeat steps 3 through 7 for the first document listed (978-0-596-52926-0).

Figure 2-4. Adding a formats field to a document using Futon

For reference, the JSON representation of our first book document with the new formats field is:

```
{
    "_id":"978-0-596-15589-6",
    "_rev":"1-3a3fa1795fda0b9004849c3199f8b104",
    "title":"CouchDB: The Definitive Guide",
    "subtitle":"Time to Relax",
    "authors":[
        "J. Chris Anderson",
        "Jan Lehnardt",
        "Noah Slater"
    ],
    "publisher":"O'Reilly Media",
```

```
      "released":"2010-01-19",
      "pages":272,
      "formats":[
         "Print",
         "Ebook",
         "Safari Books Online"
      ]
   }
```

The JSON representation of our second book document with the new formats field is:

```
{
   "_id":"978-0-596-52926-0",
   "_rev":"1-15e130dea4f192e26a6deb71974b7e51",
   "title":"RESTful Web Services",
   "subtitle":"Web services for the real world",
   "authors":[
      "Leonard Richardson",
      "Sam Ruby"
   ],
   "publisher":"O'Reilly Media",
   "released":"2007-05-08",
   "pages":448,
   "formats":[
      "Print",
      "Ebook",
      "Safari Books Online"
   ]
}
```

Update the first book using cURL instead, if you'd prefer:

```
curl -X PUT http://localhost:5984/books/978-0-596-15589-6 -d \
"{
   \"_id\":\"978-0-596-15589-6\",
   \"_rev\":\"1-3a3fa1795fda0b9004849c3199f8b104\",
   \"title\":\"CouchDB: The Definitive Guide\",
   \"subtitle\":\"Time to Relax\",
   \"authors\":[
      \"J. Chris Anderson\",
      \"Jan Lehnardt\",
      \"Noah Slater\"
   ],
   \"publisher\":\"O'Reilly Media\",
   \"released\":\"2010-01-19\",
   \"pages\":272,
   \"formats\":[
      \"Print\",
      \"Ebook\",
      \"Safari Books Online\"
   ]
}"
```

Map | 13

When updating a document, CouchDB requires the correct document revision number as part of its *Multi-Version Concurrency Control* (MVCC). This form of *optimistic concurrency* ensures that another client hasn't modified the document since you last retrieved it. If you have at all deviated from the previous steps, you may get a document update conflict when trying to modify these documents. If this happens, you will need to change the value of the _rev field in your request. You can find the current _rev value by performing a GET request on each document's URL. Revision numbers are comprised of an N- prefix indicating the number of times the document has been updated, followed by an MD5 hash of the document. Revision numbers are also used by CouchDB during replication.

The response:

```
{"ok":true,"id":"978-0-596-15589-6","rev":"2-099d205cbb59d989700ad7692cbb3e66"}
```

Update the second book using cURL:

```
curl -X PUT http://localhost:5984/books/978-0-596-52926-0 -d \
"{
    \"_id\":\"978-0-596-52926-0\",
    \"_rev\":\"1-15e130dea4f192e26a6deb71974b7e51\",
    \"title\":\"RESTful Web Services\",
    \"subtitle\":\"Web services for the real world\",
    \"authors\":[
        \"Leonard Richardson\",
        \"Sam Ruby\"
    ],
    \"publisher\":\"O'Reilly Media\",
    \"released\":\"2007-05-08\",
    \"pages\":448,
    \"formats\":[
        \"Print\",
        \"Ebook\",
        \"Safari Books Online\"
    ]
}"
```

The response:

```
{"ok":true,"id":"978-0-596-52926-0","rev":"2-de467b329baf6259e791b830cc950ece"}
```

Now let's add a third book document that is only available in Print format. Add the following document using Futon:

```
{
    "_id":"978-1-565-92580-9",
    "title":"DocBook: The Definitive Guide",
    "authors":[
        "Norman Walsh",
        "Leonard Muellner"
    ],
    "publisher":"O'Reilly Media",
```

```
    "formats":[
        "Print"
    ],
    "released":"1999-10-28",
    "pages":648
}
```

Or add the document using cURL:

```
curl -X PUT http://localhost:5984/books/978-1-565-92580-9 -d \
"{
    \"_id\":\"978-1-565-92580-9\",
    \"title\":\"DocBook: The Definitive Guide\",
    \"authors\":[
        \"Norman Walsh\",
        \"Leonard Muellner\"
    ],
    \"publisher\":\"O'Reilly Media\",
    \"formats\":[
        \"Print\"
    ],
    \"released\":\"1999-10-28\",
    \"pages\":648
}"
```

The response:

```
{"ok":true,"id":"978-1-565-92580-9","rev":"1-b945cb4799a1ccdd1689eae0e44124f1"}
```

Next, we'll write a new Map function that will give us all of the available formats for our three books. Run the following Map function in a temporary view using Futon (shown in Figure 2-5):

```
function(doc) {
    if (doc.formats) {
        for (var i in doc.formats) {
            emit(doc.formats[i]);
        }
    }
}
```

Or run the temporary view using cURL:

```
curl -X POST http://localhost:5984/books/_temp_view \
-H "Content-Type: application/json" \
-d \
'{
    "map": "function(doc) {
        if (doc.formats) {
            for (var i in doc.formats) {
                emit(doc.formats[i]);
            }
        }
    }"
}'
```

Map | 15

Figure 2-5. Creating a temporary view of book formats using Futon

The response to the cURL temporary view is:

```
{
    "total_rows":7,
    "offset":0,
    "rows":[
        {
            "id":"978-0-596-15589-6",
            "key":"Ebook",
            "value":null
        },
        {
            "id":"978-0-596-52926-0",
            "key":"Ebook",
            "value":null
        },
        {
            "id":"978-0-596-15589-6",
            "key":"Print",
            "value":null
        },
        {
            "id":"978-0-596-52926-0",
            "key":"Print",
            "value":null
        },
        {
```

```
          "id":"978-1-565-92580-9",
          "key":"Print",
          "value":null
      },
      {

          "id":"978-0-596-15589-6",
          "key":"Safari Books Online",
          "value":null
      },
      {

          "id":"978-0-596-52926-0",
          "key":"Safari Books Online",
          "value":null
      }
    ]
  }
```

See Table 2-3 for the rows in tabular format.

Table 2-3. Rows from the formats temporary view

key	id	value
"Ebook"	"978-0-596-15589-6"	null
"Ebook"	"978-0-596-52926-0"	null
"Print"	"978-0-596-15589-6"	null
"Print"	"978-0-596-52926-0"	null
"Print"	"978-1-565-92580-9"	null
"Safari Books Online"	"978-0-596-15589-6"	null
"Safari Books Online"	"978-0-596-52926-0"	null

 In Chapter 4 we'll see how to select specific ranges from your view and how to group by keys. This could be useful in finding books of only a specified format, or for finding out how many books are available in each format, for example. We'll also see how to reverse the output to be in descending order, and how to group by levels of keys.

Our book documents each have multiple authors. A view of authors may be useful as well. Run the following Map function in a temporary view using Futon (shown in Figure 2-6):

```
function(doc) {
    if (doc.authors) {
        for (var i in doc.authors) {
            emit(doc.authors[i]);
        }
    }
}
```

Map | 17

Figure 2-6. Creating a temporary view of book authors using Futon

Or run the temporary view using cURL:

```
curl -X POST http://localhost:5984/books/_temp_view \
-H "Content-Type: application/json" \
-d \
'{
    "map": "function(doc) {
        if (doc.authors) {
            for (var i in doc.authors) {
                emit(doc.authors[i]);
            }
        }
    }"
}'
```

The response to this temporary view is:

```
{
    "total_rows":7,
    "offset":0,
    "rows":[
        {
            "id":"978-0-596-15589-6",
            "key":"J. Chris Anderson",
            "value":null
        },
        {
```

```
        "id":"978-0-596-15589-6",
        "key":"Jan Lehnardt",
        "value":null
    },
    {
        "id":"978-1-565-92580-9",
        "key":"Leonard Muellner",
        "value":null
    },
    {
        "id":"978-0-596-52926-0",
        "key":"Leonard Richardson",
        "value":null
    },
    {
        "id":"978-0-596-15589-6",
        "key":"Noah Slater",
        "value":null
    },
    {
        "id":"978-1-565-92580-9",
        "key":"Norman Walsh",
        "value":null
    },
    {
        "id":"978-0-596-52926-0",
        "key":"Sam Ruby",
        "value":null
    }
  ]
}
```

See Table 2-4 for the rows in tabular format.

Table 2-4. Rows from the authors temporary view

key	id	value
"J. Chris Anderson"	"978-0-596-15589-6"	null
"Jan Lehnardt"	"978-0-596-15589-6"	null
"Leonard Muellner"	"978-1-565-92580-9"	null
"Leonard Richardson"	"978-0-596-52926-0"	null
"Noah Slater"	"978-0-596-15589-6"	null
"Norman Walsh"	"978-1-565-92580-9"	null
"Sam Ruby"	"978-0-596-52926-0"	null

Map | 19

Conclusion

You have a tremendous amount of flexibility in controlling how documents are mapped. While CouchDB supports temporary views for development work, ad hoc queries of more than a handful of documents are not practical. In Chapter 3 we'll see how to permanently save views inside of *design documents*.

Using a relational database, you can write arbitrary SQL queries against your data. With CouchDB, you must know ahead of time what data you're going to want to query. As with all technology decisions, there are trade-offs. In a relational database, each row must follow a rigid schema, yet documents in CouchDB are schema-less. Using a relational database, you can index your data to make your queries more efficient, but you can also query against nonindexed data. Mapped data in CouchDB is stored in a B-tree (technically a B+ tree) index, effectively making it impossible to query nonindexed data (other than with temporary views).

 Map functions must not have any side effects. They must only emit a key/value pair or pairs (or emit nothing) and must not interact with any state outside of its inputs and outputs. They must be deterministic, meaning that, given the same input, they will always return the same output. This means, for example, that you must not use data from a random number generator within your Map functions.

Reduce

The Map step generates a set of key/value pairs which can then optionally be reduced to a single value—or to a grouping of values—in the Reduce step. As previously discussed, the Map step generates rows that each contain the id of the mapped document, an optional key, and an optional value. The Reduce step primarily involves working with the keys and values, not document IDs. Either a single computed reduction of all values will be produced, or reductions of values grouped by keys will ultimately be produced. Grouping is controlled by parameters passed to your view, not by the Reduce function itself.

CouchDB has three built-in Reduce functions: _count, _sum, and _stats (shown in Table 2-5). In most situations, you will want to use one of these built-in Reduce functions. You can write your own custom Reduce functions, but you should rarely need to. Both the _sum and _stats built-in Reduce functions will only reduce sets of numbers. The _count function will count arbitrary values, including null values.

Table 2-5. Built-in Reduce functions

Function	Output
_count	Returns the number of mapped values in the set
_sum	Returns the sum of the set of mapped values
_stats	Returns numerical statistics of the mapped values in the set including the sum, count, min, and max

Count

The built-in _count Reduce function will likely be the most common Reduce function you use. Since it counts arbitrary values, including null values, you can use it while still leaving out the value parameter in your calls to the emit function. Let's take a look at some examples of using the built-in _count Reduce function.

Enter our formats Map function again as a temporary view in Futon:

```
function(doc) {
    if (doc.formats) {
        for (var i in doc.formats) {
            emit(doc.formats[i]);
        }
    }
}
```

This time, enter the name of the built-in _count Reduce function in the "Reduce Function" text box:

```
_count
```

Next, click "Run", check the "Reduce" checkbox (if it is not already checked), and select "none" from the "Grouping" drop-down menu. See Figure 2-7.

Or run the temporary view using cURL:

```
curl -X POST http://localhost:5984/books/_temp_view \
-H "Content-Type: application/json" \
-d \
'{
    "map": "function(doc) {
        if (doc.formats) {
            for (var i in doc.formats) {
                emit(doc.formats[i]);
            }
        }
    }",
    "reduce": "_count"
}'
```

Figure 2-7. Creating a temporary view of book formats using Futon with a reduce and no grouping

The response to this temporary view is:

```
{
    "rows":[
        {
            "key":null,
            "value":7
        }
    ]
}
```

See Table 2-6 for the row in tabular format.

Table 2-6. Reduced row from the formats temporary view with no grouping

key	value
null	7

This tells us that there is a total of seven formats within the three books in our database. Since this counts all values as opposed to values grouped by keys, the key is null.

It might be more useful to know how many books are available in each format. In Futon, change the "Grouping" drop-down menu value from "none" to "exact". This tells CouchDB to group on exact keys, as shown in Figure 2-8. It's possible to tell CouchDB to group on only parts of keys, but this is only useful if your keys are JSON arrays.

Figure 2-8. Creating a temporary view of book formats using Futon with a reduce and exact grouping

Or, using cURL:

```
curl -X POST http://localhost:5984/books/_temp_view?group=true \
-H "Content-Type: application/json" \
-d \
'{
    "map": "function(doc) {
        if (doc.formats) {
            for (var i in doc.formats) {
                emit(doc.formats[i]);
            }
        }
    }",
    "reduce": "_count"
}'
```

As you may have guessed, the group query string parameter controls whether or not to group. Using CouchDB's HTTP API, the default group_level is exact, so this parameter can be omitted. In fact, the only way to specify exact is to omit the group_level parameter, as only integers are allowed for this parameter's value. We'll explore both the group and group_level parameters in more detail in Chapter 4.

The response:

```
{
    "rows":[
        {
            "key":"Ebook",
            "value":2
        },
        {
            "key":"Print",
            "value":3
        },
        {
            "key":"Safari Books Online",
            "value":2
        }
    ]
}
```

See Table 2-7 for the rows in tabular format.

Table 2-7. Reduced rows from the formats temporary view with grouping

key	value
"Ebook"	2
"Print"	3
"Safari Books Online"	2

Here we can see that there are two books available in Ebook format, three books available in Print, and two books available on Safari Books Online. This is much more useful information.

Sum

The built-in _sum Reduce function will return a sum of mapped values. As with all reductions, you can either get a sum of all values or a sum of values grouped by keys (or parts of keys). Again, this is controlled by how you query your view, not in your Map function itself. Since _sum requires all mapped values to be numbers, let's modify our formats Map function to emit the number of pages in each book as the value.

Enter our updated formats Map function as a temporary view in Futon:

```
function(doc) {
    if (doc.formats) {
        for (var i in doc.formats) {
            emit(doc.formats[i], doc.pages);
        }
    }
}
```

Enter the name of the built-in _sum Reduce function in the "Reduce Function" text box:

```
_sum
```

Click "Run", make sure that "Reduce" is checked, and select "exact" from the "Grouping" drop-down menu. See Figure 2-9.

Figure 2-9. Creating a temporary view of book formats using Futon with a sum reduce and exact grouping

Or run the updated temporary view using cURL:

```
curl -X POST http://localhost:5984/books/_temp_view?group=true \
-H "Content-Type: application/json" \
-d \
'{
   "map": "function(doc) {
      if (doc.formats) {
         for (var i in doc.formats) {
            emit(doc.formats[i], doc.pages);
         }
      }
   }",
   "reduce": "_sum"
}'
```

The response to this temporary view is:

```
{
    "rows":[
        {
            "key":"Ebook",
            "value":720
        },
        {
            "key":"Print",
            "value":1368
        },
        {
            "key":"Safari Books Online",
            "value":720
        }
    ]
}
```

See Table 2-8 for the rows in tabular format.

Table 2-8. Reduced rows from the formats temporary view with grouping

key	value
"Ebook"	720
"Print"	1368
"Safari Books Online"	720

We see that there are a total of 720 pages of reading available in Ebook format, 1368 pages of reading available in Print format, and 720 pages of reading available on Safari Books Online.

Stats

The built-in _stats Reduce function returns a JSON object containing the sum, count, minimum, maximum, and sum over all square roots of mapped values. Enter the same Map function as before as a temporary view in Futon:

```
function(doc) {
    if (doc.formats) {
        for (var i in doc.formats) {
            emit(doc.formats[i], doc.pages);
        }
    }
}
```

Enter the name of the built-in _stats Reduce function in the "Reduce Function" text box:

```
_stats
```

Click "Run", make sure that "Reduce" is checked, and select "exact" from the "Grouping" drop-down menu (see Figure 2-10).

Or run the updated temporary view using cURL:

```
curl -X POST http://localhost:5984/books/_temp_view?group=true \
-H "Content-Type: application/json" \
-d \
'{
   "map": "function(doc) {
       if (doc.formats) {
           for (var i in doc.formats) {
               emit(doc.formats[i], doc.pages);
           }
       }
   }",
   "reduce": "_stats"
}'
```

Figure 2-10. Creating a temporary view of book formats using Futon with a stats reduce and exact grouping

The response to the temporary view:

```
{
    "rows":[
        {
            "key":"Ebook",
            "value":{
                "sum":720,
```

```
              "count":2,
              "min":272,
              "max":448,
              "sumsqr":274688
         }
    },
    {
         "key":"Print",
         "value":{
              "sum":1368,
              "count":3,
              "min":272,
              "max":648,
              "sumsqr":694592
         }
    },
    {
         "key":"Safari Books Online",
         "value":{
              "sum":720,
              "count":2,
              "min":272,
              "max":448,
              "sumsqr":274688
         }
    }
  ]
}
```

See Table 2-9 for the rows in tabular format.

Table 2-9. Reduced rows from the formats temporary view with grouping

key	value
"Ebook"	{"sum":720,"count":2,"min":272,"max":448,"sumsqr":274688}
"Print"	{"sum":1368,"count":3,"min":272,"max":648,"sumsqr":694592}
"Safari Books Online"	{"sum":720,"count":2,"min":272,"max":448,"sumsqr":274688}

Custom Reduce Functions

 The built-in Reduce functions should serve your needs most, if not all, of the time. If you find yourself writing a custom Reduce function, please take a step back and make sure that one of the built-in Reduce functions won't serve your needs better.

Here is the skeleton of a custom Reduce function:

```
function(keys, values, rereduce) {
}
```

The `keys` parameter is an array of mapped key and document IDs, with each array element being in the form [`key,id`], where `id` is the document ID. The `values` parameter is an array of mapped values. You will likely work mainly with the `values` parameter, and the goal will typically be to Reduce it to a single scalar value. The third parameter, `rereduce`, tells your function whether it is being called recursively on its own output. If `rereduce` is `true`, the `keys` parameter will be null.

CouchDB will optimize the calls to your Reduce function. If the Map step generates a small number of rows, your Reduce function may only be called once with all of the mapped rows passed in. If a large number of rows are generated in the Map step, CouchDB may call your Reduce function multiple times with seemingly arbitrary batches of rows passed in each time. The results of this batch processing will be passed to your Reduce function again, this time with `rereduce` set to `true`.

For reference, here is what a custom Reduce function that is equivalent to the built-in `_count` Reduce function would look like:

```
function(keys, values, rereduce) {
    if (rereduce) {
        return sum(values);
    } else {
        return values.length;
    }
}
```

Here is what a custom Reduce function that is equivalent to the built-in `_sum` Reduce function would look like:

```
function(keys, values, rereduce) {
    return sum(values);
}
```

 As with Map functions, a Reduce function must not have any side effects, must not interact with any state outside of its inputs and outputs, and must be deterministic. Reduce functions must not cross-reference adjacent documents—leave this to the client querying your views.

Limitations of MapReduce

While very powerful and applicable to a wide variety of problems, MapReduce is not the answer to every problem. The index generated in the Map step is one dimensional, and the Reduce step must not generate a large amount of data or there will be a serious performance degradation. For example, CouchDB's MapReduce may not be a good fit for full-text indexing or ad hoc searching. This is a problem better suited for a tool such as Lucene. Fortunately, you can integrate CouchDB with Lucene using couchdb-lucene (*https://github.com/rnewson/couchdb-lucene*), or by integrating ElasticSearch (*https://github.com/elasticsearch/elasticsearch*) and CouchDB. Indexing and searching geospatial data is also not easily done within CouchDB, but is possible using a CouchDB extension called GeoCouch (*https://github.com/couchbase/geocouch*).

CHAPTER 3

Design Documents

As we saw in Chapter 2, a MapReduce view is comprised of a Map JavaScript function and an optional Reduce JavaScript function. These functions can be run within a temporary view or they can be saved permanently as a view within a *design document*. Design documents are stored in your database alongside your other documents and can contain one or more views. They can be created, read, updated, and deleted, just like any other document. One difference between design documents and regular documents is that the ID of design documents must always begin with _design, followed by a forward slash (/), and then an identifier specific to the design document.

Titles View

Let's save a slightly updated version of our titles view from Chapter 2 to a new design document with an ID of _design/default. We'll map book documents to key/value pairs of titles and number of pages.

In Futon, navigate to the books database, select "Temporary view..." from the "View" drop-down menu, and paste the following JavaScript function into the "Map Function" text box, replacing the existing function:

```
function(doc) {
    if (doc.title) {
        emit(doc.title, doc.pages);
    }
}
```

Enter the name of the built-in _stats Reduce function in the "Reduce Function" text box:

```
_stats
```

Next, let's test your Map and Reduce functions. Click "Run", check or uncheck the "Reduce" checkbox as you'd like, and select "none" or "exact" from the "Grouping" drop-down menu. When you have verified that the output is as you'd expect, click the "Save As..." button. Enter **default** as the "Design Document" name, enter **titles** as the "View Name", and then click the "Save" button. See Figure 3-1.

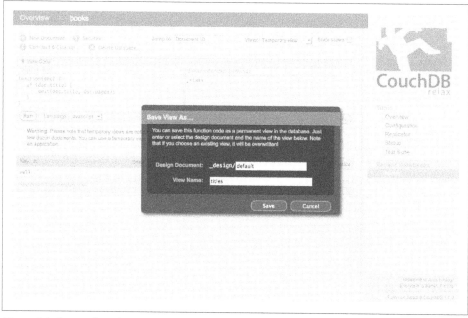

Figure 3-1. Saving the titles view in the default design document using Futon

Alternatively, you can create the default design document containing the titles view using cURL:

```
curl -X PUT http://localhost:5984/books/_design/default -d \
'{
    "_id": "_design/default",
    "language": "javascript",
    "views": {
        "titles": {
            "map":
"function(doc) {
    if (doc.title) {
        emit(doc.title, doc.pages);
    }
}",
            "reduce": "_stats"
        }
    }
}'
```

The response:

```
{"ok":true,"id":"_design/default","rev":"1-de853739dd890563bcaeb4a2309e02e5"}
```

To query this view from within Futon, select "titles" from the "View" drop-down menu under "default" (if you're not already there), check the "Reduce" checkbox (if it's not already checked), and select "none" from the "Grouping" drop-down menu. You can click the ▶ arrow next to "View Code" if you'd like to see the Map and Reduce functions that define the view. See Figure 3-2.

Figure 3-2. Querying the titles view in the default design document using Futon

To query this new view from cURL:

```
curl -X GET http://localhost:5984/books/_design/default/_view/titles
```

The response:

```
{
    "rows":[
        {
            "key":null,
            "value":{
                "sum":1368,
                "count":3,
                "min":272,
                "max":648,
                "sumsqr":694592
            }
        }
    ]
}
```

See Table 3-1 for the row in tabular format.

Table 3-1. Reduced row from the titles view with no grouping

key	value
null	{"sum":1368,"count":3,"min":272,"max":648,"sumsqr":694592}

Formats View

Next, let's save our formats view from Chapter 2 to our new _design/default design document. In this view we will map book documents to key/value pairs of formats and number of pages.

In Futon, select "Temporary view..." from the "View" drop-down menu, and paste the following function into the "Map Function" text box, replacing the existing function:

```
function(doc) {
    if (doc.formats) {
        for (var i in doc.formats) {
            emit(doc.formats[i], doc.pages);
        }
    }
}
```

Enter the name of the built-in _stats Reduce function in the "Reduce Function" text box:

```
_stats
```

Run the temporary view if you'd like, and then click the "Save As..." button. Enter **default** as the "Design Document", enter **formats** as the "View Name", and then click the "Save" button (see Figure 3-3).

Alternatively, you can update the default design document to add the formats view using cURL:

```
curl -X PUT http://localhost:5984/books/_design/default -d \
'{
  "_id": "_design/default",
  "_rev": "1-de853739dd890563bcaeb4a2309e02e5",
  "language": "javascript",
  "views": {
      "titles": {
          "map":
"function(doc) {
    if (doc.title) {
        emit(doc.title, doc.pages);
    }
}",
          "reduce": "_stats"
      },
      "formats": {
          "map":
```

```
"function(doc) {
    if (doc.formats) {
        for (var i in doc.formats) {
            emit(doc.formats[i], doc.pages);
        }
    }
}",
            "reduce": "_stats"
        }
    }
}'
```

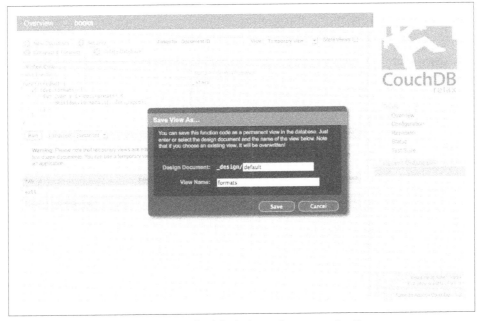

Figure 3-3. Saving the formats view in the default design document using Futon

The response:

```
{"ok":true,"id":"_design/default","rev":"2-cf88b785f94f2ddc1f9148f425f54f0d"}
```

To query this view from within Futon, select "formats" from the "View" drop-down menu under "default" (if you're not already there), check the "Reduce" checkbox (if it's not already checked), and select "none" from the "Grouping" drop-down menu. See Figure 3-4.

To query this new view from cURL:

```
curl -X GET http://localhost:5984/books/_design/default/_view/formats
```

The response:

```
{
    "rows":[
```

```
{
    "key":null,
    "value":{
        "sum":2808,
        "count":7,
        "min":272,
        "max":648,
        "sumsqr":1243968
    }
}
]
}
```

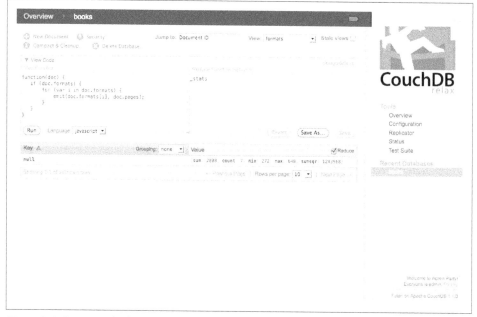

Figure 3-4. Querying the formats view in the default design document using Futon

See Table 3-2 for the row in tabular format.

Table 3-2. Reduced row from the formats view with no grouping

key	value
null	{"sum":2808,"count":7,"min":272,"max":648,"sumsqr":1243968}

Authors View

Finally, let's save our authors view from Chapter 2 to our new _design/default design document. In this view we will map book documents to key/value pairs of authors and number of pages.

In Futon, select "Temporary view…" from the "View" drop-down menu, and paste the following function into the "Map Function" text box, replacing the existing function:

```
function(doc) {
    if (doc.authors) {
        for (var i in doc.authors) {
            emit(doc.authors[i], doc.pages);
        }
    }
}
```

Enter the name of the built-in _stats Reduce function in the "Reduce Function" text box:

```
_stats
```

Run the temporary view if you'd like, and then click the "Save As…" button. Enter **default** again as the "Design Document", enter **authors** as the "View Name", and then click the "Save" button. See Figure 3-5.

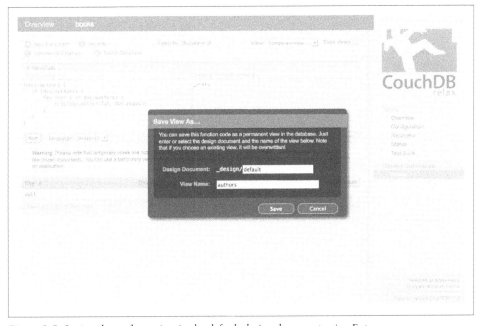

Figure 3-5. Saving the authors view in the default design document using Futon

Alternatively, you can update the **default** design document to add the authors view using cURL:

```
curl -X PUT http://localhost:5984/books/_design/default -d \
'{
    "_id": "_design/default",
    "_rev": "2-cf88b785f94f2ddc1f9148f425f54f0d",
    "language": "javascript",
```

```
    "views": {
        "titles": {
            "map":
    "function(doc) {
        if (doc.title) {
            emit(doc.title, doc.pages);
        }
    }",
            "reduce": "_stats"
        },
        "formats": {
            "map":
    "function(doc) {
        if (doc.formats) {
            for (var i in doc.formats) {
                emit(doc.formats[i], doc.pages);
            }
        }
    }",
            "reduce": "_stats"
        },
        "authors": {
            "map":
    "function(doc) {
        if (doc.authors) {
            for (var i in doc.authors) {
                emit(doc.authors[i], doc.pages);
            }
        }
    }",
            "reduce": "_stats"
        }
    }
}'
```

The response:

```
{"ok":true,"id":"_design/default","rev":"3-9f27b209caab2d19cf07aac6d406568c"}
```

To query this view from within Futon, select "authors" from the "View" drop-down menu under "default" (if you're not already there), check the "Reduce" checkbox (if it's not already checked), and select "none" from the "Grouping" drop-down menu (shown in Figure 3-6).

To query this new view from cURL:

```
curl -X GET http://localhost:5984/books/_design/default/_view/authors
```

The response:

```
{
    "rows":[
        {
            "key":null,
            "value":{
                "sum":3008,
```

```
            "count":7,
            "min":272,
            "max":648,
            "sumsqr":1463168
        }
      }
    ]
  }
```

Figure 3-6. Querying the authors view in the default design document using Futon

See Table 3-3 for the row in tabular format.

Table 3-3. Reduced row from the authors view with no grouping

key	value
null	{"sum":3008,"count":7,"min":272,"max":648,"sumsqr":1463168}

Storage Considerations

The examples in this book involve using only a handful of views, each with a handful of rows. You will want to consider the storage implications of the views in you database as you will likely have more views, each with more rows. CouchDB views use extra disk space in exchange for additional performance and for concurrency purposes. Some benefits of this approach are that huge amounts of data can be accessed very quickly and that your data can always be read, even when your database is being written to, but you will want to carefully choose and design your views in order to preserve disk space.

Each view in your database is stored as its own B-tree index. CouchDB views can be written to without blocking read operations. Write operations are serialized, but concurrent read operations are allowed. CouchDB will provide a consistent view of the database to each and every read operation. This is achieved by only ever appending to the B-tree file on each update. The one exception to this append-only rule is the part of the file containing the B-tree root node, which *is* overwritten on each update. Existing parts of the file are never changed (except for the part containing the B-tree root node) and file pointers to an old B-tree root node will still provide a consistent, if possibly outdated, snapshot of the database. This append-only design can lead to large index files. See the CouchDB Wiki page on Compaction (*http://wiki.apache.org/couchdb/ Compaction*) for information on how to compact and clean up views. For more details on how B-trees are implemented in CouchDB, see *CouchDB: The Definitive Guide* (*http://oreilly.com/catalog/9780596155902*), Part 6: Appendixes, Appendix F: The Power of B-trees.

CHAPTER 4

Querying Views

In Chapter 3 we saw how to save views to a design document. Now that you have created views, you can query the data that is held in them. Here are several of the things you can do when querying views in CouchDB:

- If a Reduce function is defined for your view, you can specify whether to reduce the results.
- You can query for all rows within a view, a single contiguous range of rows within a view, or even a row or rows matching a specified key within a view. You *cannot* query for multiple ranges.
- You can limit results to a specified number of rows, and you can specify a number of rows to be skipped.
- You can return results in ascending or descending order.
- You can group rows by keys or by parts of keys.
- You can ask CouchDB to include the original document with each row from which that row was emitted.
- You can tell CouchDB that you're OK with *stale* results. This means that CouchDB may not refresh any of the view's data, potentially giving you outdated results. This option can be used to improve performance.

When querying views from Futon, you can choose whether to run the Reduce step. If the Reduce step is run, you can choose whether you want grouping, and whether the grouping should be based on the "exact" key or only part of the key. Results are paginated, so Futon effectively lets you limit and skip rows in your results. Futon lets you reverse the order of results. Futon also lets you tell CouchDB that you're OK with stale results.

The current version of Futon doesn't let you specify a range for your query, nor does it allow you to ask CouchDB to include the original document in your results, although Futon does provide a hyperlink to a representation of that document. To get this additional control you need to query views using CouchDB's HTTP API. You can do this using cURL, so most of the examples in this chapter will only be provided in cURL.

Your view query options are controlled by query parameters added to your view's URL. See Table 4-1 for a list of available query parameters. All parameters are optional.

Table 4-1. View query options

Parameter	Description
reduce	If a Reduce function is defined, this parameter lets you choose whether or not to run the Reduce step. The default value is true.
startkey	A URL encoded JSON value indicating the key at which to start the range.
start key_docid	The ID of the document with which to start the range. This parameter is, for all intents and purposes, ignored if it is not used in conjunction with the startkey parameter. CouchDB will first look at the startkey parameter and then use the startkey_docid parameter to further refine the beginning of the range if multiple potential starting rows have the same key but different document IDs.
endkey	A URL encoded JSON value indicating the key at which to end the range.
endkey_docid	The ID of the document with which to end the range. This parameter is, for all intents and purposes, ignored if it is not used in conjunction with the endkey parameter. CouchDB will first look at the endkey parameter and then use the endkey_docid parameter to further refine the end of the range if multiple potential ending rows have the same key but different document IDs.
inclusive_end	Indicates whether to include the endkey and endkey_docid (if set) in the range. The default value is true.
key	A URL encoded JSON value indicating an exact key on which to match.
limit	The maximum number or rows to include in the output.
skip	The number of rows to skip. The default value is 0.
descending	Indicates whether to reverse the output to be in descending order. The default value is false. This option is applied before rows are filtered, so you will likely need to swap your startkey/start key_docid and endkey/endkey_docid parameter values.
group	Indicates whether to group results by keys. This parameter can only be true if a Reduce function is defined for your view and the reduce parameter is set to true (its default). The default value of this parameter is false.
group_level	If your keys are JSON arrays, this parameter will specify how many elements in those arrays to use for grouping purposes. If your keys are not JSON arrays, this parameter's value will effectively be ignored.
include_docs	Indicates whether to fetch the original document from which the row was emitted. This parameter can only be true if a Reduce function is *not* defined for your view, *or* the reduce parameter is set to false. The default value of this parameter is false.
stale	Set the value of this parameter to ok if you are OK with possibly getting outdated results. Set the value to update_after if you are OK with possibly getting outdated results, but would like to trigger a view update after your results have been retrieved.

Range Queries

A range query allows you to control resultant rows by starting and/or ending key and, optionally, document ID. If no startkey or endkey is defined, all rows from the view will be included in your results. You can also specify an exact key on which to match.

Rows by Start and End Keys

Let's get a list of authors whose names begin with the letter "j":

The `--data-urlencode` switch was added to cURL in version 7.18.0. If you are using a version of cURL that is older than 7.18.0, you will need to replace the `--data-urlencode` switch with the `-d` switch and manually URL encode the data on the right side of the equals sign. You can find out which version of cURL you are using by running `curl -V`. Check out Eric Meyer's online URL Decoder/Encoder (*http://meyerweb.com/eric/tools/dencoder/*). To apply this to the example to follow, you could replace `--data-urlencode startkey='"j"'` with `-d startkey='%22j%22'`, and replace `--data-urlencode endkey='"j\ufff0"'` with `-d endkey='%22j%5Cufff0%22'`.

```
curl -X GET http://localhost:5984/books/_design/default/_view/authors -G \
-d reduce=false \
--data-urlencode startkey=\
'"j"' \
--data-urlencode endkey=\
'"j\ufff0"'
```

As you may remember, string comparison in CouchDB is implemented according to the Unicode Collation Algorithm. This has a couple of practical implications when you are searching for a range of strings. Strings are case sensitive, and the lower case version of a letter will sort before the upper case version. This is why we used a lower case "j" instead of an upper case "J" as the `startkey` in the previous example. We could have used "jz" as the `endkey`, but `\ufff0` represents a high value unicode character. Using "j\ufff0" as the `endkey` ensures that we account for non-Latin characters.

The response:

```
{
    "total_rows":7,
    "offset":0,
    "rows":[
        {
            "id":"978-0-596-15589-6",
            "key":"J. Chris Anderson",
            "value":272
        },
        {
            "id":"978-0-596-15589-6",
            "key":"Jan Lehnardt",
            "value":272
        }
    ]
}
```

See Table 4-2 for the rows in tabular format.

Table 4-2. Rows from the authors view, filtered by start and end keys

key	id	value
"J. Chris Anderson"	"978-0-596-15589-6"	272
"Jan Lehnardt"	"978-0-596-15589-6"	272

You can optionally use cURL's -v switch to see the details of the request:

```
curl -v -X GET http://localhost:5984/books/_design/default/_view/authors -G \
-d reduce=false \
--data-urlencode startkey=\
'"J"' \
--data-urlencode endkey=\
'"J\ufff0"'
```

This will let you see that cURL is URL encoding the JSON values for you:

```
?reduce=false&startkey=%22J%22&endkey=%22J%5Cufff0%22
```

Rows by Key

Let's get a book format by key:

```
curl -X GET http://localhost:5984/books/_design/default/_view/formats -G \
-d reduce=false \
--data-urlencode key=\
'"Print"'
```

The response:

```
{
   "total_rows":7,
   "offset":2,
   "rows":[
      {
         "id":"978-0-596-15589-6",
         "key":"Print",
         "value":272
      },
      {
         "id":"978-0-596-52926-0",
         "key":"Print",
         "value":448
      },
      {
         "id":"978-1-565-92580-9",
         "key":"Print",
         "value":648
      }
   ]
}
```

See Table 4-3 for the rows in tabular format.

Table 4-3. Rows from the formats view, filtered by key

key	id	value
"Print"	"978-0-596-15589-6"	272
"Print"	"978-0-596-52926-0"	448
"Print"	"978-1-565-92580-9"	648

Let's see the same query reduced:

```
curl -X GET http://localhost:5984/books/_design/default/_view/formats -G \
--data-urlencode key=\
'"Print"'
```

The response:

```
{
    "rows":[
        {
            "key":null,
            "value":{
                "sum":1368,
                "count":3,
                "min":272,
                "max":648,
                "sumsqr":694592
            }
        }
    ]
}
```

See Table 4-4 for the row in tabular format.

Table 4-4. Reduced row from the formats view with no grouping, filtered by key

key	value
null	{"sum":1368,"count":3,"min":272,"max":648,"sumsqr":694592}

Rows by Start and End Keys and Document IDs

Let's get a list of book formats within a range of keys and document IDs. If you remember, the document IDs are the books' ISBNs:

```
curl -X GET http://localhost:5984/books/_design/default/_view/formats -G \
-d reduce=false \
--data-urlencode startkey=\
'"Ebook"' \
--data-urlencode startkey_docid=\
'978-0-596-52926-0' \
--data-urlencode endkey=\
'"Print"' \
--data-urlencode endkey_docid=\
'978-0-596-52926-0'
```

The response:

```
{
    "total_rows":7,
    "offset":1,
    "rows":[
        {
            "id":"978-0-596-52926-0",
            "key":"Ebook",
            "value":448
        },
        {
            "id":"978-0-596-15589-6",
            "key":"Print",
            "value":272
        },
        {
            "id":"978-0-596-52926-0",
            "key":"Print",
            "value":448
        }
    ]
}
```

See Table 4-5 for the rows in tabular format.

Table 4-5. Rows from the formats view, filtered by start and end keys and document IDs

key	id	value
"Ebook"	"978-0-596-52926-0"	448
"Print"	"978-0-596-15589-6"	272
"Print"	"978-0-596-52926-0"	448

 The actual key in CouchDB's B-tree index is not just the key emitted from your Map function, but a combination of the key and the document's ID. You may have multiple rows with the same key in a view, as is the case with the book formats view. The `startkey_docid` and `endkey_docid` parameters allow you to be more specific about the starting and ending rows of your range. Think of the `startkey_docid` parameter as a way to add specificity to the `startkey` parameter, and the `endkey_docid` parameter as a way to add specificity to the `endkey` parameter.

Limiting, Skipping, and Reversing Results

CouchDB allows you to limit the number of results returned, skip an arbitrary number of results, and reverse the output of results to be in descending order.

Limit

Let's query for all book formats, but limit the number of results to five:

```
curl -X GET http://localhost:5984/books/_design/default/_view/formats -G \
-d reduce=false \
-d limit=5
```

The response:

```
{
    "total_rows":7,
    "offset":0,
    "rows":[
        {
            "id":"978-0-596-15589-6",
            "key":"Ebook",
            "value":272
        },
        {
            "id":"978-0-596-52926-0",
            "key":"Ebook",
            "value":448
        },
        {
            "id":"978-0-596-15589-6",
            "key":"Print",
            "value":272
        },
        {
            "id":"978-0-596-52926-0",
            "key":"Print",
            "value":448
        },
        {
            "id":"978-1-565-92580-9",
            "key":"Print",
            "value":648
        }
    ]
}
```

See Table 4-6 for the rows in tabular format.

Table 4-6. Rows from the formats view, limited to five

key	id	value
"Ebook"	"978-0-596-15589-6"	272
"Ebook"	"978-0-596-52926-0"	448
"Print"	"978-0-596-15589-6"	272
"Print"	"978-0-596-52926-0"	448
"Print"	"978-1-565-92580-9"	648

Skip

Let's query for all book formats, limit the number of results to five again, but this time let's skip the first five results:

```
curl -X GET http://localhost:5984/books/_design/default/_view/formats -G \
-d reduce=false \
-d limit=5 \
-d skip=5
```

The response:

```
{
    "total_rows":7,
    "offset":5,
    "rows":[
        {
            "id":"978-0-596-15589-6",
            "key":"Safari Books Online",
            "value":272
        },
        {
            "id":"978-0-596-52926-0",
            "key":"Safari Books Online",
            "value":448
        }
    ]
}
```

See Table 4-7 for the rows in tabular format.

Table 4-7. Rows from the formats view, limited to five and skipping the first five results

key	id	value
"Safari Books Online"	"978-0-596-15589-6"	272
"Safari Books Online"	"978-0-596-52926-0"	448

 The skip parameter can be used along with the limit parameter to implement pagination. However, skipping a large number of rows can be inefficient. Instead, set the skip parameter's value to 1 and use the key of the last row on the previous page as the startkey (endkey if output is reversed) parameter, and the document ID of the last row on the previous page as the startkey_docid (endkey_docid if output is reversed) parameter. This should give you better performance since CouchDB will not need to scan the entire range of skipped rows.

Following best practices, let's instead set the skip parameter's value to 1 and use the startkey and startkey_docid parameters:

```
curl -X GET http://localhost:5984/books/_design/default/_view/formats -G \
-d reduce=false \
-d limit=5 \
-d skip=1 \
```

```
--data-urlencode startkey=\
'"Print"' \
--data-urlencode startkey_docid=\
'978-1-565-92580-9' \
-d limit=5
```

The response:

```
{
    "total_rows":7,
    "offset":5,
    "rows":[
        {
            "id":"978-0-596-15589-6",
            "key":"Safari Books Online",
            "value":272
        },
        {
            "id":"978-0-596-52926-0",
            "key":"Safari Books Online",
            "value":448
        }
    ]
}
```

See Table 4-8 for the rows in tabular format.

Table 4-8. Rows from the formats view, limited to five and filtered by start key and document ID

key	id	value
"Safari Books Online"	"978-0-596-15589-6"	272
"Safari Books Online"	"978-0-596-52926-0"	448

Reversing Output

Let's reverse the output of our book titles view:

```
curl -X GET http://localhost:5984/books/_design/default/_view/titles -G \
-d reduce=false \
-d descending=true
```

The response:

```
{
    "total_rows":3,
    "offset":0,
    "rows":[
        {
            "id":"978-0-596-52926-0",
            "key":"RESTful Web Services",
            "value":448
        },
        {
            "id":"978-1-565-92580-9",
            "key":"DocBook: The Definitive Guide",
```

```
          "value":648
        },
        {
          "id":"978-0-596-15589-6",
          "key":"CouchDB: The Definitive Guide",
          "value":272
        }
      ]
    }
```

See Table 4-9 for the rows in tabular format.

Table 4-9. Rows from the titles view in descending order

key	id	value
"RESTful Web Services"	"978-0-596-52926-0"	448
"DocBook: The Definitive Guide"	"978-1-565-92580-9"	648
"CouchDB: The Definitive Guide"	"978-0-596-15589-6"	272

> If you set the descending parameter's value to true, you will likely have to swap your startkey/startkey_docid and/or endkey/endkey_docid parameter values, if used. This is because the output is reversed before rows are filtered.

Grouping

CouchDB allows you to group by exact keys or by parts of keys. With exact grouping, your keys can be arbitrary JSON values. To group by parts of keys, your keys must be JSON arrays.

Exact Grouping

Let's get a list of authors whose names begin with the letter "j" again, this time reduced:

```
curl -X GET http://localhost:5984/books/_design/default/_view/authors -G \
--data-urlencode startkey=\
'"j"' \
--data-urlencode endkey=\
'"j\ufff0"'
```

The response:

```
{
    "rows":[
        {
            "key":null,
            "value":{
                "sum":544,
                "count":2,
                "min":272,
                "max":272,
```

```
            "sumsqr":147968
          }
        }
      }
    ]
  }
```

See Table 4-10 for the row in tabular format.

Table 4-10. Reduced row from the authors view with no grouping, filtered by start and end keys

key	value
null	{"sum":544,"count":2,"min":272,"max":272,"sumsqr":147968}

Now let's see this query grouped by key:

```
curl -X GET http://localhost:5984/books/_design/default/_view/authors -G \
-d group=true \
--data-urlencode startkey=\
'"j"' \
--data-urlencode endkey=\
'"j\ufff0"'
```

The response:

```
{
  "rows":[
    {
      "key":"J. Chris Anderson",
      "value":{
        "sum":272,
        "count":1,
        "min":272,
        "max":272,
        "sumsqr":73984
      }
    },
    {
      "key":"Jan Lehnardt",
      "value":{
        "sum":272,
        "count":1,
        "min":272,
        "max":272,
        "sumsqr":73984
      }
    }
  ]
}
```

See Table 4-11 for the rows in tabular format.

Table 4-11. Reduced rows from the authors view, grouped and filtered by start and end keys

key	value
"J. Chris Anderson"	{"sum":272,"count":1,"min":272,"max":272,"sumsqr":73984}
"Jan Lehnardt"	{"sum":272,"count":1,"min":272,"max":272,"sumsqr":73984}

Group Levels

Let's create a new view that allows us to see when books were released by year, month, and day. We will call this the releases view and add it to our _design/default design document. In this new view, we will map book documents to key/value pairs of release dates and number of pages. Instead of a string, the release date will be a JSON array containing the date's year, month, and day. We will do this by using the split method of JavaScript's String object on each book document's released field. If we split a string representation of a date, e.g., 2007-05-08, by the "-" character, we end up with a JSON array, e.g., ["2007","05","08"]. Group levels require JSON arrays to group on, and they work best when the array elements are ordered from least specific to most specific. Our date example meets these criteria because it is a JSON array with the first element representing the year (least specific), the second element representing the month (more specific), and the third element representing the day (most specific).

For this example, let's add a fourth book document that was published in January 2010, the same year and month as *CouchDB: The Definitive Guide* (*http://oreilly.com/catalog/9780596155902/*). Add the following document using Futon:

```
{
    "_id":"978-0-596-80579-1",
    "title":"Building iPhone Apps with HTML, CSS, and JavaScript",
    "subtitle":"Making App Store Apps Without Objective-C or Cocoa",
    "authors":[
        "Jonathan Stark"
    ],
    "publisher":"O'Reilly Media",
    "formats":[
        "Print",
        "Ebook",
        "Safari Books Online"
    ],
    "released":"2010-01-08",
    "pages":192
}
```

Or add the document using cURL:

```
curl -X PUT http://localhost:5984/books/978-0-596-80579-1 -d \
"{
    \"_id\":\"978-0-596-80579-1\",
    \"title\":\"Building iPhone Apps with HTML, CSS, and JavaScript\",
    \"subtitle\":\"Making App Store Apps Without Objective-C or Cocoa\",
    \"authors\":[
        \"Jonathan Stark\"
```

```
        ],
        \"publisher\":\"O'Reilly Media\",
        \"formats\":[
           \"Print\",
           \"Ebook\",
           \"Safari Books Online\"
        ],
        \"released\":\"2010-01-08\",
        \"pages\":192
     }"
```

The response:

```
{"ok":true,"id":"978-0-596-80579-1","rev":"1-09ce09fef75068834da99957c7b14cf2"}
```

Now let's create a new view. In Futon, navigate to the books database, select "Temporary view…" from the "View" drop-down menu, and paste the following JavaScript function into the "Map Function" text box, replacing the existing function:

```
function(doc) {
  if (doc.released) {
      emit(doc.released.split("-"), doc.pages);
  }
}
```

Enter the name of the built-in _stats Reduce function in the "Reduce Function" text box:

```
_stats
```

Next test your Map and Reduce functions by clicking "Run". When you have verified that the output is as you'd expect, click the "Save As…" button. Enter **default** as the "Design Document" name, enter **releases** as the "View Name", and then click the "Save" button. See Figure 4-1.

Alternatively, you can update the default design document to add the releases view using cURL:

```
curl -X PUT http://localhost:5984/books/_design/default -d \
'{
   "_id": "_design/default",
   "_rev": "3-9f27b209caab2d19cf07aac6d406568c",
   "language": "javascript",
   "views": {
      "titles": {
          "map":
"function(doc) {
  if (doc.title) {
      emit(doc.title, doc.pages);
  }
}",
          "reduce": "_stats"
      },
      "formats": {
          "map":
"function(doc) {
```

```
    if (doc.formats) {
        for (var i in doc.formats) {
            emit(doc.formats[i], doc.pages);
        }
    }
}",
        "reduce": "_stats"
    },
    "authors": {
        "map":
"function(doc) {
    if (doc.authors) {
        for (var i in doc.authors) {
            emit(doc.authors[i], doc.pages);
        }
    }
}",
        "reduce": "_stats"
    },
    "releases": {
        "map":
"function(doc) {
    if (doc.released) {
        emit(doc.released.split(\"-\"), doc.pages);
    }
}",
        "reduce": "_stats"
    }
}'
```

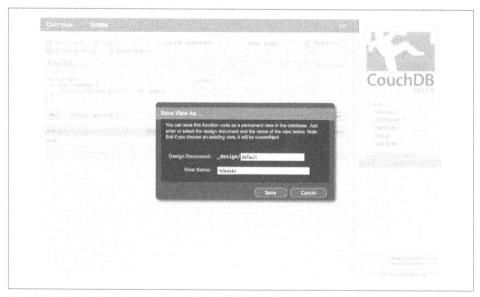

Figure 4-1. Saving the releases view in the default design document using Futon

The response:

```
{"ok":true,"id":"_design/default","rev":"4-7591c2802e00785281be2b4e408de52c"}
```

In Futon, select "releases" from the "View" drop-down menu under "default" (if you're not already there), check the "Reduce" checkbox (if it's not already checked), and select "exact" from the "Grouping" drop-down menu. See Figure 4-2.

Figure 4-2. Querying the releases view in the default design document using Futon with exact grouping

To run this same query using cURL:

```
curl -X GET http://localhost:5984/books/_design/default/_view/releases -G \
-d group=true
```

The response:

```
{
    "rows":[
        {
            "key":[
                "1999",
                "10",
                "28"
            ],
            "value":{
                "sum":648,
                "count":1,
                "min":648,
                "max":648,
                "sumsqr":419904
```

```
            }
        },
        {
            "key":[
                "2007",
                "05",
                "08"
            ],
            "value":{
                "sum":448,
                "count":1,
                "min":448,
                "max":448,
                "sumsqr":200704
            }
        },
        {
            "key":[
                "2010",
                "01",
                "08"
            ],
            "value":{
                "sum":192,
                "count":1,
                "min":192,
                "max":192,
                "sumsqr":36864
            }
        },
        {
            "key":[
                "2010",
                "01",
                "19"
            ],
            "value":{
                "sum":272,
                "count":1,
                "min":272,
                "max":272,
                "sumsqr":73984
            }
        }
    ]
}
```

See Table 4-12 for the rows in tabular format.

Table 4-12. Reduced rows from the releases view with grouping

key	value
["1999","10","28"]	{"sum":648,"count":1,"min":648,"max":648,"sumsqr":419904}
["2007","05","08"]	{"sum":448,"count":1,"min":448,"max":448,"sumsqr":200704}
["2010","01","08"]	{"sum":192,"count":1,"min":192,"max":192,"sumsqr":36864}
["2010","01","19"]	{"sum":272,"count":1,"min":272,"max":272,"sumsqr":73984}

So far this isn't a whole lot different than what we've seen before; we're still grouping by the exact keys. Next, let's group by just the year that books were released.

In Futon, select "releases" from the "View" drop-down menu under "default" (if you're not already there), check the "Reduce" checkbox (if it's not already checked), and select "level 1" from the "Grouping" drop-down menu. See Figure 4-3.

Figure 4-3. Querying the releases view in the default design document using Futon with level one grouping

To run this same query using cURL:

```
curl -X GET http://localhost:5984/books/_design/default/_view/releases -G \
-d group=true \
-d group_level=1
```

The response:

```
{
    "rows":[
        {
            "key":[
                "1999"
            ],
            "value":{
                "sum":648,
                "count":1,
                "min":648,
                "max":648,
                "sumsqr":2500
            }
        },
        {
            "key":[
                "2007"
            ],
            "value":{
                "sum":448,
                "count":1,
                "min":448,
                "max":448,
                "sumsqr":200704
            }
        },
        {
            "key":[
                "2010"
            ],
            "value":{
                "sum":464,
                "count":2,
                "min":192,
                "max":272,
                "sumsqr":110848
            }
        }
    ]
}
```

See Table 4-13 for the rows in tabular format.

Table 4-13. Reduced rows from the releases view with level one grouping

key	value
["1999"]	{"sum":648,"count":1,"min":648,"max":648,"sumsqr":419904}
["2007"]	{"sum":448,"count":1,"min":448,"max":448,"sumsqr":200704}
["2010"]	{"sum":464,"count":2,"min":192,"max":272,"sumsqr":110848}

Based on these results, we can see that in 1999 there was a total of 648 pages inside books released, 1 book was released, and the minimum and maximum pages of any book released was 648. In 2007, there was a total of 448 pages inside books released, 1 book was released, and the minimum and maximum number of pages in any book released was 448. In 2010, there was a total of 464 pages inside books released, 2 books were released, the minimum number of pages in any book released was 192, and the maximum number of pages in any book released was 272. Finally, let's group by the year and month that books were released.

In Futon, select "releases" from the "View" drop-down menu under "default" (if you're not already there), check the "Reduce" checkbox (if it's not already checked), and select "level 2" from the "Grouping" drop-down menu (see Figure 4-4).

Figure 4-4. Querying the releases view in the default design document using Futon with level two grouping

To run this same query using cURL:

```
curl -X GET http://localhost:5984/books/_design/default/_view/releases -G \
-d group=true \
-d group_level=2
```

The response:

```
{
    "rows":[
        {
            "key":[
```

```
            "1999",
            "10"
        ],
        "value":{
            "sum":648,
            "count":1,
            "min":648,
            "max":648,
            "sumsqr":419904
        }
    },
    {
        "key":[
            "2007",
            "05"
        ],
        "value":{
            "sum":448,
            "count":1,
            "min":448,
            "max":448,
            "sumsqr":200704
        }
    },
    {
        "key":[
            "2010",
            "01"
        ],
        "value":{
            "sum":464,
            "count":2,
            "min":192,
            "max":272,
            "sumsqr":110848
        }
    }
  ]
}
```

See Table 4-14 for the rows in tabular format.

Table 4-14. Reduced rows from the releases view with level two grouping

key	value
["1999","10"]	{"sum":648,"count":1,"min":648,"max":648,"sumsqr":419904}
["2007","05"]	{"sum":448,"count":1,"min":448,"max":448,"sumsqr":200704}
["2010","01"]	{"sum":464,"count":2,"min":192,"max":272,"sumsqr":110848}

We could also group by year, month, and day (a level three grouping) but—for this particular example—this would effectively be the same as an exact grouping.

Including Documents

Let's get all of our book titles, including the original documents, in the results this time:

```
curl -X GET http://localhost:5984/books/_design/default/_view/titles -G \
-d reduce=false \
-d include_docs=true
```

The response:

```json
{
    "total_rows":4,
    "offset":0,
    "rows":[
        {
            "id":"978-0-596-80579-1",
            "key":"Building iPhone Apps with HTML, CSS, and JavaScript",
            "value":192,
            "doc":{
                "_id":"978-0-596-80579-1",
                "_rev":"1-09ce09fef75068834da99957c7b14cf2",
                "title":"Building iPhone Apps with HTML, CSS, and JavaScript",
                "subtitle":"Making App Store Apps Without Objective-C or Cocoa",
                "authors":[
                    "Jonathan Stark"
                ],
                "publisher":"O'Reilly Media",
                "formats":[
                    "Print",
                    "Ebook",
                    "Safari Books Online"
                ],
                "released":"2010-01-08",
                "pages":192
            }
        },
        {
            "id":"978-0-596-15589-6",
            "key":"CouchDB: The Definitive Guide",
            "value":272,
            "doc":{
                "_id":"978-0-596-15589-6",
                "_rev":"2-099d205cbb59d989700ad7692cbb3e66",
                "title":"CouchDB: The Definitive Guide",
                "subtitle":"Time to Relax",
                "authors":[
                    "J. Chris Anderson",
                    "Jan Lehnardt",
                    "Noah Slater"
                ],
                "publisher":"O'Reilly Media",
                "released":"2010-01-19",
                "pages":272,
                "formats":[
                    "Print",
                    "Ebook",
```

```
            "Safari Books Online"
        ]
    }
},
{
    "id":"978-1-565-92580-9",
    "key":"DocBook: The Definitive Guide",
    "value":648,
    "doc":{
        "_id":"978-1-565-92580-9",
        "_rev":"1-b945cb4799a1ccdd1689eae0e44124f1",
        "title":"DocBook: The Definitive Guide",
        "authors":[
            "Norman Walsh",
            "Leonard Muellner"
        ],
        "publisher":"O'Reilly Media",
        "formats":[
            "Print"
        ],
        "released":"1999-10-28",
        "pages":648
    }
},
{
    "id":"978-0-596-52926-0",
    "key":"RESTful Web Services",
    "value":448,
    "doc":{
        "_id":"978-0-596-52926-0",
        "_rev":"2-de467b329baf6259e791b830cc950ece",
        "title":"RESTful Web Services",
        "subtitle":"Web services for the real world",
        "authors":[
            "Leonard Richardson",
            "Sam Ruby"
        ],
        "publisher":"O'Reilly Media",
        "released":"2007-05-08",
        "pages":448,
        "formats":[
            "Print",
            "Ebook",
            "Safari Books Online"
        ]
    }
}
]
}
```

See Table 4-15 for the rows in tabular format.

Table 4-15. Rows from the titles view

key	id	value	doc (**truncated**)
"Building iPhone Apps with HTML, CSS, and JavaScript"	"978-0-596-80579-1"	192	{…}
"CouchDB: The Definitive Guide"	"978-0-596-15589-6"	272	{…}
"DocBook: The Definitive Guide"	"978-1-565-92580-9"	648	{…}
"RESTful Web Services"	"978-0-596-52926-0"	448	{…}

Including documents is a very convenient feature. However, you may want to consider retrieving the documents separately. This may seem less efficient, but it gives your client the opportunity to cache individual documents. If your client has a cached version, it can make a conditional HTTP request using the cached document's ETag. If the ETag matches that of the most current revision of the document, CouchDB will respond indicating that the document has not been modified and will not send the full document. This can save bandwidth and speed up requests.

CHAPTER 5

MapReduce Views for SQL Users

Many developers who are new to CouchDB are already familiar with relational databases such as MySQL. However, there are some important differences between CouchDB and relational databases. These differences include:

- There are no tables in a CouchDB database as each document can have its own schema. Since there are no tables, there are also no columns.
- Views in CouchDB serve a similar role as indexes in a relational database. However, views/indexes are queried directly in CouchDB, whereas in a relational database indexes are used to optimize more generalized queries.
- A column in a CouchDB result set can contain a mix of logical data types. A column in a result set from a relational database will always contain the same logical data type.
- CouchDB has no built-in concept of relationships between documents.
- In CouchDB, related data can be embedded in a document, referenced from a document, or both. These design decisions have important implications.
- While CouchDB is fully ACID compliant, it does not support transactions across document boundaries.

Although CouchDB has no concept of tables, columns, or rows when it comes to documents, there is one place where columns and rows are applicable: CouchDB views. Every row in a CouchDB view (generated from a Map function) has the same three columns: `key` (from the first parameter of your call to the `emit` function), `id` (the document identifier for the document context from which the `emit` function was called), and `value` (from the second parameter to your call to the `emit` function). If you specify `include_docs=true` in your query, then CouchDB will also include a `doc` column in the result set.

The `key`, `value`, and `doc` columns can contain different logical data types in each row. For example, one row may contain data representing the name of a publisher in the `value` column and the next row may contain data representing the title of a book in the `value` column. The `id` column will always contain document identifiers.

CouchDB has no built-in concept of relationships between entities. However, there are ways to mimic entity relationships from within your views. In this chapter, we'll take a look at several patterns that you can use to create relationships between entities when using CouchDB. These patterns involve either embedding related entity data or collating referenced data across documents within a CouchDB view.

Documents

Each document in CouchDB can have a completely different structure than the next. While it's common for documents to fall into one or more categories, with documents in the same category sharing a similar schema, CouchDB does nothing to enforce this by default. For example, you may choose to have some documents represent books, other documents represent authors, and still other documents represent publishers. In a relational database, you would store books, authors, and publishers in separate tables. In CouchDB, book, author, and publisher documents would live right next to each other in the same database as CouchDB has no concept of tables.

 It is technically possible to enforce a schema through the use of document update validation functions. For more information, see the CouchDB Wiki page on Document Update Validation (*http://wiki .apache.org/couchdb/Document_Update_Validation*), or *CouchDB: The Definitive Guide* (*http://oreilly.com/catalog/9780596155902*), Part 2: Developing with CouchDB, Chapter 7: Validation Functions. While CouchDB does not enforce a schema by default, it is still important to carefully consider the design of your documents when using CouchDB.

Here is an example of a document representing a book:

```
{
    "_id":"book/9780596155896",
    "collection":"book",
    "title":"CouchDB: The Definitive Guide",
    "subtitle":"Time to Relax",
    "authors":[
        "author/3631",
        "author/3633",
        "author/3632"
    ],
    "publisher":"publisher/oreilly",
    "formats":[
        "Print",
        "Ebook",
        "Safari Books Online"
    ]
    "released":"2010-01-19",
    "pages":272
}
```

The `collection` field used in these examples is of no particular significance to CouchDB as CouchDB has no concept of collections. We will use this field in our Map functions to filter documents by type. For example, if we want to Map just books, we can filter using a conditional:

```
if ("book" == doc.collection) { emit(); }
```

Here is an example of a document representing an author:

```
{
    "_id":"author/3631",
    "collection":"author",
    "firstname":"J. Chris",
    "lastname":"Anderson"
}
```

Here is an example of a document representing a publisher:

```
{
    "_id":"publisher/oreilly",
    "collection":"publisher",
    "name":"O'Reilly Media"
}
```

None of the above "relationships" between documents have any particular meaning to CouchDB, although your application may understand the semantics of these relationships. You can also use these values to effectively create relationships when building your views, as you'll see later.

Views

The only way to query a CouchDB database (other than accessing individual documents directly) is through the use of views. Views are defined by a Map function and an optional Reduce function. Every view has exactly three columns (the `doc` column is technically not part of the view, but can optionally be returned as part of the result set):

key
> This is the first argument to the `emit` function call(s) in your Map function. Any valid JSON value is allowed. The `key` argument is optional and will be `null` in the generated view row if omitted.

id
> Whenever the `emit` function is called in a Map function, the document ID of the mapped document is automatically included as part of the generated view row.

value
> This is the second argument to the `emit` function call(s) in your Map function. Any valid JSON value is allowed. The `value` argument is optional and will be `null` in the generated view row if omitted.

Once a view has been created, CouchDB offers a variety of ways to query the view. Queries are made against the view's key field. Results can be further refined using the view's id field. All three fields are returned as part of the results and the originating document can optionally be included as well (only if results are not reduced and not grouped). If a Reduce function is defined for the view, then results can be grouped and aggregate values can be returned. See Chapter 4 for more information about querying views.

Compound Keys

Compound keys are an essential tool for querying related documents. They can be used to perform the equivalent of an SQL join, as you'll see in the next section. In a CouchDB view, a compound key is a key made up of more than one attribute. The most common type of compound key in CouchDB is a JSON array. Here is an example of a Map function that emits a compound key, as a JSON array:

```
function(doc) {
    if (doc.collection && doc.title) {
        emit([doc.collection, doc.title]);
    }
}
```

The above compound key has the effect of indexing documents first by collection, and then by title (only if the document has both a collection and a title). Later, we'll see examples of using compound keys to retrieve data from related documents.

A JSON object can serve as a compound key as well. For example:

```
function(doc) {
    if (doc.collection && doc.title) {
        emit({"collection":doc.collection, "title": doc.title});
    }
}
```

JSON objects are more expressive, but they also make the resulting index larger.

Relationships

While CouchDB has no built-in concept of relationships between documents, there are some techniques you can use to model relationships in your documents and views. The CouchDB Wiki page on Modeling Entity Relationships in CouchDB (*http://wiki.apache .org/couchdb/EntityRelationship*) and Google's Modeling Entity Relationships (*http:// code.google.com/appengine/articles/modeling.html*) article were used as a reference for this section. If you'd like to compare the following examples to a relational database, please reference the column descriptions for the publisher (Table 5-1), book (Table 5-2), author (Table 5-3), and book_author (Table 5-4).

Table 5-1. Column descriptions from the publisher table

Field	Type	Null	Key	Default	Extra
publisher_id	varchar(255)	NO	PRI	NULL	
name	varchar(255)	YES		NULL	

Table 5-2. Column descriptions from the book table

Field	Type	Null	Key	Default	Extra
book_id	varchar(255)	NO	PRI	NULL	
publisher_id	varchar(255)	YES	MUL	NULL	
title	varchar(255)	YES		NULL	
subtitle	varchar(255)	YES		NULL	
formats	set('Print','Ebook','Safari Books Online')	YES		NULL	
released	date	YES		NULL	
pages	int(10) unsigned	YES		NULL	

Table 5-3. Column descriptions from the author table

Field	Type	Null	Key	Default	Extra
author_id	varchar(255)	NO	PRI	NULL	
firstname	varchar(255)	YES		NULL	
lastname	varchar(255)	YES		NULL	

Table 5-4. Column descriptions from the book_author junction table

Field	Type	Null	Key	Default	Extra
book_id	varchar(255)	NO	PRI	NULL	
author_id	varchar(255)	NO	PRI	NULL	

 The relational database design outlined here is intended to make it easy for you to translate between the equivalent SQL and CouchDB queries. This is not necessarily a recommended database design. For example, the primary key fields should probably be integers and the fact that the formats field in the book table is defined as a set may limit your ability to query based on book formats.

There are significant differences between how entities are related in a relational database and how they can be related in CouchDB. In a relational database, sets of entities of the same type are stored in tables. For example, a set of publishers is stored in one table, and a set of books is stored in another table. If you want to query for publishers and related books, the data from both tables is "joined" together in each row of the result set (see Figure 5-1).

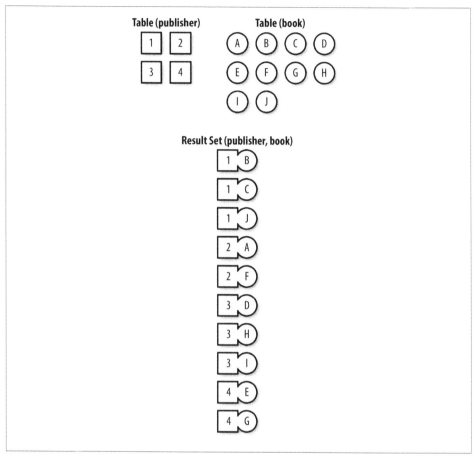

Figure 5-1. Joining data from two tables using a relational database

In a CouchDB database, there is no schema, so there are no tables. Documents of different "types" sit next to each other in the database. You cannot "join" data in the same way that you can in a relational database. However, you can collate your views such that related data will sort together (see Figure 5-2).

One to Many

With a one to many relationship, one parent object may have many related child objects. For example, a publisher will have many books. This relationship can be modeled all in one documented, or by relating multiple documents.

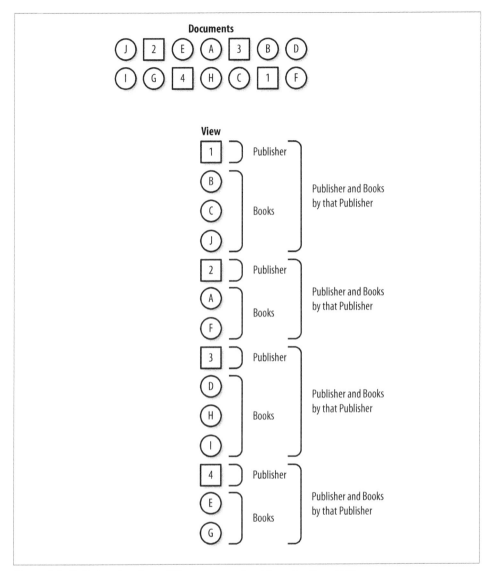

Figure 5-2. Collating data from different types of entities using CouchDB

Embedded JSON array

The simplest approach to creating a one to many relationship between entities in CouchDB is to just store all of the related data in one document. This only works if there aren't too many related entities. Too many related entities embedded in one document can result in very large documents. Large documents can be slow to transfer

between client and server, unwieldy to modify, and time-consuming to index. Here is
an example of a publisher document with its related data embedded:

```json
{
    "_id":"publisher/oreilly",
    "collection":"publisher",
    "name":"O'Reilly Media",
    "books":[
        {
            "title":"CouchDB: The Definitive Guide",
            "subtitle":"Time to Relax",
            "authors":[
                {
                    "firstname":"J. Chris",
                    "lastname":"Anderson"
                },
                {
                    "firstname":"Jan",
                    "lastname":"Lehnardt"
                },
                {
                    "firstname":"Noah",
                    "lastname":"Slater"
                }
            ],
            "formats":[
                "Print",
                "Ebook",
                "Safari Books Online"
            ],
            "released":"2010-01-19",
            "pages":272
        },
        {
            "title":"RESTful Web Services",
            "subtitle":"Web services for the real world",
            "authors":[
                {
                    "firstname":"Leonard",
                    "lastname":"Richardson"
                },
                {
                    "firstname":"Sam",
                    "lastname":"Ruby"
                }
            ],
            "formats":[
                "Print",
                "Ebook",
                "Safari Books Online"
            ],
            "released":"2007-05-08",
            "pages":448
        },
        {
```

```
        "title":"DocBook: The Definitive Guide",
        "authors":[
            {
                "firstname":"Norman",
                "lastname":"Walsh"
            },
            {
                "firstname":"Leonard",
                "lastname":"Muellner"
            }
        ],
        "formats":[
            "Print"
        ],
        "released":"1999-10-28",
        "pages":648
    },
    {
        "title":"Building iPhone Apps with HTML, CSS, and JavaScript",
        "subtitle":"Making App Store Apps Without Objective-C or Cocoa",
        "authors":[
            {
                "firstname":"Jonathan",
                "lastname":"Stark"
            }
        ],
        "formats":[
            "Print",
            "Ebook",
            "Safari Books Online"
        ],
        "released":"2010-01-08",
        "pages":192
    }
    ]
}
```

Here is an SQL query that we might use to get publishers and related books:

```
SELECT
  `publisher`.`publisher_id`,
  `publisher`.`name`,
  `book`.`title`
FROM `publisher`
LEFT JOIN `book`
  ON `publisher`.`publisher_id` = `book`.`publisher_id`
ORDER BY
  `publisher`.`publisher_id`,
  `book`.`title`;
```

To truly be equivalent to the corresponding CouchDB views, the SQL query examples throughout this chapter should use full outer joins instead of left outer joins. Not all databases support full outer joins. Full outer joins can be emulated through a union of both left and right outer joins. Using a full outer join would have made these examples not work in some databases (including MySQL). Emulating a full outer join would have made these examples more difficult to understand.

The above SQL query would give us the results outlined in Table 5-5.

Table 5-5. Rows from an SQL query of publishers and books

publisher_id	name	title
publisher/oreilly	O'Reilly Media	Building iPhone Apps with HTML, CSS, and Java Script
publisher/oreilly	O'Reilly Media	CouchDB: The Definitive Guide
publisher/oreilly	O'Reilly Media	DocBook: The Definitive Guide
publisher/oreilly	O'Reilly Media	RESTful Web Services

Here is a CouchDB Map function that would let you query for publishers' books:

```
function(doc) {
    if ("publisher" == doc.collection) {
        emit([doc._id, 0], doc.name);
        if (doc.books) {
            for (var i in doc.books) {
                emit([doc._id, 1], doc.books[i].title);
            }
        }
    }
}
```

The first emit call gives us a row in our view for the parent entity, in this case the publisher itself. This makes sure that all publishers will be listed, even if they have no books. The 0 value for the second element of the compound key gives CouchDB a low value to collate on when the first elements of the array match (i.e. when we're emitting data from the same publisher entity). This will effectively make our publisher row sort before our book rows, for an individual publisher.

The second emit call gives us a row for each book within a publisher. The 1 value for the second element of the compound key gives CouchDB a value greater than 0 to collate on when the first elements of the array match. This will effectively make our book rows sort after the associated publisher rows. Querying the view containing the above Map function gives us the results outlined in Table 5-6.

Table 5-6. Rows from a view of publishers and embedded books

key	id	value
["publisher/oreilly",0]	"publisher/oreilly"	"O'Reilly Media"
["publisher/oreilly",1]	"publisher/oreilly"	"Building iPhone Apps with HTML, CSS, and JavaScript"
["publisher/oreilly",1]	"publisher/oreilly"	"CouchDB: The Definitive Guide"
["publisher/oreilly",1]	"publisher/oreilly"	"DocBook: The Definitive Guide"
["publisher/oreilly",1]	"publisher/oreilly"	"RESTful Web Services"

As you can see, the first row returned represents the publisher—the equivalent of the left side of a join in SQL. The next three rows represent each related book—the equivalent of the right side of a join in SQL. If our database contained more than one publisher, we could have gotten the books for this one single publisher by specifying a startkey of ["publisher/oreilly"], and an endkey of ["publisher/oreilly",{}].

> If CouchDB's querying capabilities seem limiting, it's for a good reason. Unlike a relational database, CouchDB *only* lets you query for indexed data. This is an intentional decision in the design of CouchDB as it only allows you to make efficient queries. However, it does mean that sometimes you either need to make more than one query to get all of the needed data, or duplicate data in multiple documents.

Unlike an SQL query result, there are separate rows for the left and right sides of the join. Also unlike an SQL query result, there are different logical data types returned within the same column. The first row for the value column represents the name of a publisher, while the second, third, and fourth rows for the value column represents the title of a book. An SQL query result would never contain varying logical data types within the same column.

Related documents

As you might have guessed, storing all of a publisher's data in one document is probably not a good idea as a publisher could have *many* books. You could instead store the data for each book in its own document. Splitting up data into multiple documents reduces the probability of document update conflicts. It can also reduce the amount of redundant data. However, CouchDB does not support transactions across document boundaries. This means that inconsistencies can be introduced between a publisher's data and its related book data. The decision between using an embedded JSON array or using related documents depends on your application's requirements. Here is an example of a publisher document that does not contain related author data:

```
{
    "_id":"publisher/oreilly",
    "collection":"publisher",
    "name":"O'Reilly Media"
}
```

The first related book document:

```
{
    "_id":"book/9780596155896",
    "collection":"book",
    "title":"CouchDB: The Definitive Guide",
    "subtitle":"Time to Relax",
    "authors":[
        {
            "firstname":"J. Chris",
            "lastname":"Anderson"
        },
        {
            "firstname":"Jan",
            "lastname":"Lehnardt"
        },
        {
            "firstname":"Noah",
            "lastname":"Slater"
        }
    ],
    "publisher":"publisher/oreilly",
    "formats":[
        "Print",
        "Ebook",
        "Safari Books Online"
    ],
    "released":"2010-01-19",
    "pages":272
}
```

The second related book document:

```
{
    "_id":"book/9780596529260",
    "collection":"book",
    "title":"RESTful Web Services",
    "subtitle":"Web services for the real world",
    "authors":[
        {
            "firstname":"Leonard",
            "lastname":"Richardson"
        },
        {
            "firstname":"Sam",
            "lastname":"Ruby"
        }
    ],
    "publisher":"publisher/oreilly",
    "formats":[
        "Print",
```

```
        "Ebook",
        "Safari Books Online"
    ],
    "released":"2007-05-08",
    "pages":448
}
```

The third related book document:

```
{
    "_id":"book/9781565925809",
    "collection":"book",
    "title":"DocBook: The Definitive Guide",
    "authors":[
        {
            "firstname":"Norman",
            "lastname":"Walsh"
        },
        {
            "firstname":"Leonard",
            "lastname":"Muellner"
        }
    ],
    "publisher":"publisher/oreilly",
    "formats":[
        "Print"
    ],
    "released":"1999-10-28",
    "pages":648
}
```

The fourth related book document:

```
{
    "_id":"book/9780596805791",
    "collection":"book",
    "title":"Building iPhone Apps with HTML, CSS, and JavaScript",
    "subtitle":"Making App Store Apps Without Objective-C or Cocoa",
    "authors":[
        {
            "firstname":"Jonathan",
            "lastname":"Stark"
        }
    ],
    "publisher":"publisher/oreilly",
    "formats":[
        "Print",
        "Ebook",
        "Safari Books Online"
    ],
    "released":"2010-01-08",
    "pages":192
}
```

Here is an SQL query that we might use to get publishers and related books:

```
SELECT
  `publisher`.`publisher_id`,
  `publisher`.`name`,
  `book`.`book_id`,
  `book`.`title`
FROM `publisher`
LEFT JOIN `book`
  ON `publisher`.`publisher_id` = `book`.`publisher_id`
ORDER BY
  `publisher`.`publisher_id`,
  `book`.`book_id`;
```

The above SQL query would give us the results outlined in Table 5-7.

Table 5-7. Rows from an SQL query of publishers and books, with book identifiers

publisher_id	name	book_id	title
publisher/oreilly	O'Reilly Media	book/9780596155896	CouchDB: The Definitive Guide
publisher/oreilly	O'Reilly Media	book/9780596529260	RESTful Web Services
publisher/oreilly	O'Reilly Media	book/9780596805791	Building iPhone Apps with HTML, CSS, and JavaScript
publisher/oreilly	O'Reilly Media	book/9781565925809	DocBook: The Definitive Guide

Here is the Map function that would let you query for publishers' books when using related documents:

```
function(doc) {
    if ("publisher" == doc.collection) {
        emit([doc._id, 0], doc.name);
    }
    if ("book" == doc.collection) {
        emit([doc.publisher, 1], doc.title);
    }
}
```

Querying the view containing the above Map function gives us the results outlined in Table 5-8.

Table 5-8. Rows from a view of publishers and related books

key	id	value
["publisher/oreilly",0]	"publisher/oreilly"	"O'Reilly Media"
["publisher/oreilly",1]	"book/9780596155896"	"CouchDB: The Definitive Guide"
["publisher/oreilly",1]	"book/9780596529260"	"RESTful Web Services"

key	id	value
["publisher/oreilly",1]	"book/9780596805791"	"Building iPhone Apps with HTML, CSS, and JavaScript"
["publisher/oreilly",1]	"book/9781565925809"	"DocBook: The Definitive Guide"

Just like before, if our database contained more than one publisher, we could have gotten the books for this one single publisher by specifying a startkey of ["publisher/oreilly"], and an endkey of ["publisher/oreilly",{}].

Many to Many

Sometimes you may need to model many to many relationships. For example, each book can have multiple authors and each author can have multiple books.

List of keys

The simplest approach to creating a many to many relationship between entities in CouchDB is to store a list of keys on one side of the relationship. We will take a look at storing references on one side of the relationship, and then the other. We will see what your options are when the references aren't stored on the side of the relationship needed to let you query for the related data that you would like to access. We will also briefly discuss the possibility of storing references on both sides of the relationship, and the potential problems that come along with this.

Books and related author data. In order to query for books and related author data, we will embed references to books within each author. The first book:

```
{
    "_id":"book/9781565925809",
    "collection":"book",
    "title":"DocBook: The Definitive Guide",
    "publisher":"publisher/oreilly",
    "formats":[
        "Print"
    ],
    "released":"1999-10-28",
    "pages":648
}
```

A second book, which shares an author with the first book:

```
{
    "_id":"book/9780596805029",
    "collection":"book",
    "title":"DocBook 5: The Definitive Guide",
    "publisher":"publisher/oreilly",
    "formats":[
        "Print",
        "Ebook",
```

```
        "Safari Books Online"
    ],
    "released":"2010-04-20",
    "pages":550
}
```

A third book, which also shares an author with the first book:

```
{
    "_id":"book/9781565920514",
    "collection":"book",
    "title":"Making TeX Work",
    "publisher":"publisher/oreilly",
    "formats":[
        "Print"
    ],
    "released":"1994-04-01",
    "pages":522
}
```

The first related author document, with embedded book references:

```
{
    "_id":"author/364",
    "collection":"author",
    "firstname":"Norman",
    "lastname":"Walsh",
    "books":[
        "book/9780596805029",
        "book/9781565925809",
        "book/9781565920514"
    ]
}
```

The second related author document, with embedded book references:

```
{
    "_id":"author/748",
    "collection":"author",
    "firstname":"Leonard",
    "lastname":"Muellner",
    "books":[
        "book/9781565925809"
    ]
}
```

Here is an SQL query that we might use to get books and related authors:

```
SELECT
  `book`.`book_id`,
  `book`.`title`,
  `author`.`author_id`,
  CONCAT(`author`.`firstname`, ' ', `author`.`lastname`) AS `name`
FROM `book`
LEFT JOIN `book_author`
  ON `book`.`book_id` = `book_author`.`book_id`
LEFT JOIN `author`
  ON `book_author`.`author_id` = `author`.`author_id`
```

```
ORDER BY
    `book`.`book_id`,
    `author`.`author_id`;
```

The above SQL query would give us the results outlined in Table 5-9.

Table 5-9. Rows from an SQL query of books and related authors

book_id	title	author_id	name
book/9780596805029	DocBook 5: The Definitive Guide	author/364	Norman Walsh
book/9781565920514	Making TeX Work	author/364	Norman Walsh
book/9781565925809	DocBook: The Definitive Guide	author/364	Norman Walsh
book/9781565925809	DocBook: The Definitive Guide	author/748	Leonard Muellner

Here is a Map function that would let you query for a book's authors and get data from both book and author entities:

```
function(doc) {
    if ("book" == doc.collection) {
        emit([doc._id, 0], doc.title);
    }
    if ("author" == doc.collection) {
        if (doc.books) {
            for (var i in doc.books) {
                emit([doc.books[i], 1], doc.firstname + " " + doc.lastname);
            }
        }
    }
}
```

Querying the view containing the above Map function gives us the results outlined in Table 5-10.

Table 5-10. Rows from a view of books and related authors

key	id	value
["book/9780596805029",0]	"book/9780596805029"	"DocBook 5: The Definitive Guide"
["book/9780596805029",1]	"author/364"	"Norman Walsh"
["book/9781565920514",0]	"book/9781565920514"	"Making TeX Work"
["book/9781565920514",1]	"author/364"	"Norman Walsh"
["book/9781565925809",0]	"book/9781565925809"	"DocBook: The Definitive Guide"
["book/9781565925809",1]	"author/364"	"Norman Walsh"
["book/9781565925809",1]	"author/748"	"Leonard Muellner"

We can get the authors for a single book—let's say "DocBook: The Definitive Guide", for example—by specifying a startkey of ["book/9781565925809"], and an endkey of ["book/9781565925809",{}].

Authors and related book data. In order to query for authors and related book data, we will embed references to authors within each book. An updated version of the the first book, now with embedded author references:

 When deciding which side of the relationship on which to store the references, you'll likely want to store the list of keys on the side of the relationship with the fewest references. For example, a book is likely to have fewer authors than an author has books. If this is the case, you may want to store a list of author references in books, but not store the list of book references in authors.

```
{
    "_id":"book/9781565925809",
    "collection":"book",
    "title":"DocBook: The Definitive Guide",
    "authors":[
        "author/364",
        "author/748"
    ],
    "publisher":"publisher/oreilly",
    "formats":[
        "Print"
    ],
    "released":"1999-10-28",
    "pages":648
}
```

An updated version of the second book, now with an embedded author reference:

```
{
    "_id":"book/9780596805029",
    "collection":"book",
    "title":"DocBook 5: The Definitive Guide",
    "authors":[
        "author/364"
    ],
    "publisher":"publisher/oreilly",
    "formats":[
        "Print",
        "Ebook",
        "Safari Books Online"
    ],
    "released":"2010-04-20",
    "pages":550
}
```

An updated version of the third book, now with an embedded author reference:

```
{
    "_id":"book/9781565920514",
    "collection":"book",
    "title":"Making TeX Work",
    "authors":[
        "author/364"
    ],
    "publisher":"publisher/oreilly",
    "formats":[
        "Print"
    ],
    "released":"1994-04-01",
    "pages":522
}
```

The first related author document, now without embedded book references:

```
{
    "_id":"author/364",
    "collection":"author",
    "firstname":"Norman",
    "lastname":"Walsh"
}
```

The second related author document, now without embedded book references:

```
{
    "_id":"author/748",
    "collection":"author",
    "firstname":"Leonard",
    "lastname":"Muellner"
}
```

Here is an SQL query that we might use to get authors and related books:

```sql
SELECT
    `author`.`author_id`,
    CONCAT(`author`.`firstname`, ' ', `author`.`lastname`) AS `name`,
    `book`.`book_id`,
    `book`.`title`
FROM `author`
LEFT JOIN `book_author`
    ON `author`.`author_id` = `book_author`.`author_id`
LEFT JOIN `book`
    ON `book_author`.`book_id` = `book`.`book_id`
ORDER BY
    `author`.`author_id`,
    `book`.`book_id`;
```

The above SQL query would give us the results outlined in Table 5-11.

Table 5-11. Rows from an SQL query of authors and related books

author_id	name	book_id	title
author/364	Norman Walsh	book/9780596805029	DocBook 5: The Definitive Guide
author/364	Norman Walsh	book/9781565920514	Making TeX Work
author/364	Norman Walsh	book/9781565925809	DocBook: The Definitive Guide
author/748	Leonard Muellner	book/9781565925809	DocBook: The Definitive Guide

Here is a Map function that would let you query for an author's books and get data from both author and book entities:

```
function(doc) {
    if ("author" == doc.collection) {
        emit([doc._id, 0], doc.firstname + " " + doc.lastname);
    }
    if ("book" == doc.collection) {
        if (doc.authors) {
            for (var i in doc.authors) {
                emit([doc.authors[i], 1], doc.title);
            }
        }
    }
}
```

Querying the view containing the above Map function gives us the results outlined in Table 5-12.

Table 5-12. Rows from a view of authors and related books

key	id	value
["author/364",0]	"author/364"	"Norman Walsh"
["author/364",1]	"book/9780596805029"	"DocBook 5: The Definitive Guide"
["author/364",1]	"book/9781565920514"	"Making TeX Work"
["author/364",1]	"book/9781565925809"	"DocBook: The Definitive Guide"
["author/748",0]	"author/748"	"Leonard Muellner"
["author/748",1]	"book/9781565925809"	"DocBook: The Definitive Guide"

We could have gotten the books for a single author—let's say "Norman Walsh", for example—by specifying a startkey of ["author/364"], and an endkey of ["author/364", {}].

Books and related author references. If books have an embedded list of authors, but authors do not have an embedded list of books, it is still possible to query for books and related author references.

Here is an SQL query that we might use to get books and related author references:

```sql
SELECT
    `book`.`book_id`,
    `book`.`title`,
    `book_author`.`author_id`
FROM `book`
LEFT JOIN `book_author`
    ON `book`.`book_id` = `book_author`.`book_id`
ORDER BY
    `book`.`book_id`,
    `book_author`.`author_id`;
```

The above SQL query would give us the results outlined in Table 5-13.

Table 5-13. Rows from an SQL query of books and related author identifiers

book_id	title	author_id
book/9780596805029	DocBook 5: The Definitive Guide	author/364
book/9781565920514	Making TeX Work	author/364
book/9781565925809	DocBook: The Definitive Guide	author/364
book/9781565925809	DocBook: The Definitive Guide	author/748

Here is the Map function that lets us query for books and related author references if books have an embedded list of authors, but authors do not have an embedded list of books:

```javascript
function(doc) {
    if ("book" == doc.collection) {
        emit([doc._id, 0], doc.title);
        if (doc.authors) {
            for (var i in doc.authors) {
                emit([doc._id, 1], {"_id":doc.authors[i]});
            }
        }
    }
}
```

Querying the view containing the above Map function gives us the results outlined in Table 5-14.

Table 5-14. Rows from a view of books and related authors, with author identifiers only

key	id	value
["book/9780596805029",0]	"book/9780596805029"	"DocBook 5: The Definitive Guide"
["book/9780596805029",1]	"book/9780596805029"	{"_id":"author/364"}
["book/9781565920514",0]	"book/9781565920514"	"Making TeX Work"
["book/9781565920514",1]	"book/9781565920514"	{"_id":"author/364"}

key	id	value
["book/9781565925809",0]	"book/9781565925809"	"DocBook: The Definitive Guide"
["book/9781565925809",1]	"book/9781565925809"	{"_id":"author/364"}
["book/9781565925809",1]	"book/9781565925809"	{"_id":"author/748"}

You'll notice that these results are very similar to the results from an earlier view that we looked at. The big difference is that we were not able to include data from the author documents in our view results. Instead, we included the document identifiers for the author documents within the value column, with which we can make additional requests to the database for required data.

 With many of these examples, you can set the include_docs parameter to true in your query to retrieve the entire document as part of the result set. When the identifier is returned as the value, this is only possible if you emit a JSON object containing a key of _id with a value of the related document's identifier (as is done in these examples). This overrides the default behavior of the document from which the row was emitted being included when the include_docs parameter is set to true, and instead includes the document having an identifier matching the value of the _id key.

Authors and related book references. If authors have an embedded list of books, but books do not have an embedded list of authors, it is still possible to query for authors and related book references.

Here is an SQL query that we might use to get authors and related book references:

```
SELECT
  `author`.`author_id`,
  CONCAT(`author`.`firstname`, ' ', `author`.`lastname`) AS `name`,
  `book_author`.`book_id`
FROM `author`
LEFT JOIN `book_author`
  ON `author`.`author_id` = `book_author`.`author_id`
ORDER BY
  `author`.`author_id`,
  `book_author`.`book_id`;
```

The above SQL query would give us the results outlined in Table 5-15.

Table 5-15. Rows from an SQL query of authors and related book identifiers

author_id	name	book_id
author/364	Norman Walsh	book/9780596805029
author/364	Norman Walsh	book/9781565920514
author/364	Norman Walsh	book/9781565925809

author_id	name	book_id
author/748	Leonard Muellner	book/9781565925809

Here is the Map function that lets us query for authors and related book references if authors have an embedded list of books, but books do not have an embedded list of authors:

```
function(doc) {
    if ("author" == doc.collection) {
        emit([doc._id, 0], doc.firstname + " " + doc.lastname);
        if (doc.books) {
            for (var i in doc.books) {
                emit([doc._id, 1], {"_id":doc.books[i]});
            }
        }
    }
}
```

Querying the view containing the above Map function gives us the results outlined in Table 5-16.

Table 5-16. Rows from a view of authors and related books, with book identifiers only

key	id	value
["author/364",0]	"author/364"	"Norman Walsh"
["author/364",1]	"author/364"	{"_id":"book/ 9780596805029"}
["author/364",1]	"author/364"	{"_id":"book/ 9781565920514"}
["author/364",1]	"author/364"	{"_id":"book/ 9781565925809"}
["author/748",0]	"author/748"	"Leonard Muellner"
["author/748",1]	"author/748"	{"_id":"book/ 9781565925809"}

If you want the ability to query for related data in both directions, you could store references in both directions. However, there are a couple of potential problems with this approach. First, for entities with many relationships, a large number of references can result in large documents. As mentioned earlier, large documents can be slow to transfer between client and server, unwieldy to modify, and time-consuming to index. Second, storing references on both sides of the relationship can be complicated to maintain and, if not properly managed, can result in data anomalies. For example, inconsistent document updates could result in a relationship being represented in one direction, but not the other. Depending on which view you queried, the relationship may or may not represented.

Relationship document

For many to many relationships with a large number of entities on both ends of the relationship, using a relationship document may be the best option. A relationship document can also be helpful if the relationships between entities are updated often and are causing document update conflicts when replicating. A relationship document is similar in concept to a junction table in a relational database. Neither entity stores a reference to the other entity, but instead each relationship gets its own document. Following are examples of what book, author, and relationship entities might look.

The first book, "DocBook: The Definitive Guide":

```
{
    "_id":"book/9781565925809",
    "collection":"book",
    "title":"DocBook: The Definitive Guide",
    "publisher":"publisher/oreilly",
    "formats":[
        "Print"
    ],
    "released":"1999-10-28",
    "pages":648
}
```

The second book, "DocBook 5: The Definitive Guide":

```
{
    "_id":"book/9780596805029",
    "collection":"book",
    "title":"DocBook 5: The Definitive Guide",
    "publisher":"publisher/oreilly",
    "formats":[
        "Print",
        "Ebook",
        "Safari Books Online"
    ],
    "released":"2010-04-20",
    "pages":550
}
```

The third book, "Making TeX Work":

```
{
    "_id":"book/9781565920514",
    "collection":"book",
    "title":"Making TeX Work",
    "publisher":"publisher/oreilly",
    "formats":[
        "Print"
    ],
    "released":"1994-04-01",
    "pages":522
}
```

The first author, "Norman Walsh":

```
{
    "_id":"author/364",
    "collection":"author",
    "firstname":"Norman",
    "lastname":"Walsh"
}
```

The second author, "Leonard Muellner":

```
{
    "_id":"author/748",
    "collection":"author",
    "firstname":"Leonard",
    "lastname":"Muellner"
}
```

A document that represents a relationship from "DocBook: The Definitive Guide" to "Norman Walsh":

```
{
    "_id":"book/9781565925809/author/364",
    "collection":"book-author",
    "book":"book/9781565925809",
    "author":"author/364"
}
```

The document identifiers used throughout these examples are intended to make the example documents, and corresponding view output, easier to read. However, you may *not* want to model the naming convention for your document identifiers after those used in these examples. Your entities may have a more natural key that would make sense to use as document identifiers. You may want to consider using UUIDs generated by CouchDB, especially for relationship documents.

There are potential performance considerations when choosing your document identifiers, especially with large data sets. CouchDB will perform best with document IDs that are mostly monotonic (in simpler terms, mostly sequential). This has to do with the B+tree structure that CouchDB uses to store data. The simplest way to generate mostly monotonic document IDs is to use the default value of `sequential` for the `algorithm` option in the `uuids` configuration section of your CouchDB server and let CouchDB generate your document IDs.

A document that represents a relationship from "DocBook: The Definitive Guide" to "Leonard Muellner":

```
{
    "_id":"book/9781565925809/author/748",
    "collection":"book-author",
    "book":"book/9781565925809",
    "author":"author/748"
}
```

A document that represents a relationship from "DocBook 5: The Definitive Guide" to "Norman Walsh":

```
{
    "_id":"book/9780596805029/author/364",
    "collection":"book-author",
    "book":"book/9780596805029",
    "author":"author/364"
}
```

A document that represents a relationship from "Making TeX Work" to "Norman Walsh":

```
{
    "_id":"book/9781565920514/author/364",
    "collection":"book-author",
    "book":"book/9781565920514",
    "author":"author/364"
}
```

Books and related authors. Here is an SQL query that we might use to get books and related authors:

```
SELECT
  `book`.`book_id`,
  `book`.`title`,
  `book_author`.`author_id`
FROM `book`
LEFT JOIN `book_author`
  ON `book`.`book_id` = `book_author`.`book_id`
ORDER BY
  `book`.`book_id`,
  `book_author`.`author_id`;
```

The above SQL query would give us the results outlined previously in Table 5-13.

Here is the Map function that would let you query for a book's authors when using related documents:

```
function(doc) {
    if ("book" == doc.collection) {
        emit([doc._id, 0], doc.title);
    }
    if ("book-author" == doc.collection) {
        emit([doc.book, 1], {"_id":doc.author});
    }
}
```

Querying the view containing the above Map function gives us the results outlined in Table 5-17.

Table 5-17. Rows from a view of books and related authors, using relationship documents

key	id	value
["book/9780596805029",0]	"book/9780596805029"	"DocBook 5: The Definitive Guide"
["book/9780596805029",1]	"book/9780596805029/ author/364"	{"_id":"author/364"}
["book/9781565920514",0]	"book/9781565920514"	"Making TeX Work"
["book/9781565920514",1]	"book/9781565920514/ author/364"	{"_id":"author/364"}
["book/9781565925809",0]	"book/9781565925809"	"DocBook: The Definitive Guide"
["book/9781565925809",1]	"book/9781565925809/ author/364"	{"_id":"author/364"}
["book/9781565925809",1]	"book/9781565925809/ author/748"	{"_id":"author/748"}

Just like before, we can get the authors for a single book—let's say "DocBook: The Definitive Guide", for example—by specifying a startkey of ["book/9781565925809"], and an endkey of ["book/9781565925809",{}].

Authors and related books. Here is an SQL query that we might use to get authors and related books:

```
SELECT
  `author`.`author_id`,
  CONCAT(`author`.`firstname`, ' ', `author`.`lastname`) AS `name`,
  `book_author`.`book_id`
FROM `author`
LEFT JOIN `book_author`
  ON `author`.`author_id` = `book_author`.`author_id`
ORDER BY
  `author`.`author_id`,
  `book_author`.`book_id`;
```

The above SQL query would give us the results outlined previously in Table 5-15.

Here is the Map function that would let you query for an author's books when using related documents:

```
function(doc) {
    if ("author" == doc.collection) {
        emit([doc._id, 0], doc.firstname + " " + doc.lastname);
    }
    if ("book-author" == doc.collection) {
        emit([doc.author, 1], {"_id":doc.book});
    }
}
```

Querying the view containing the above Map function gives us the results outlined in Table 5-18.

Table 5-18. Rows from a view of authors and related books, using relationship documents

key	id	value
["author/364",0]	"author/364"	"Norman Walsh"
["author/364",1]	"book/9780596805029/author/364"	{"_id":"book/9780596805029"}
["author/364",1]	"book/9781565920514/author/364"	{"_id":"book/9781565920514"}
["author/364",1]	"book/9781565925809/author/364"	{"_id":"book/9781565925809"}
["author/748",0]	"author/748"	"Leonard Muellner"
["author/748",1]	"book/9781565925809/author/748"	{"_id":"book/9781565925809"}

Just like before, we could have gotten the books for a single author—let's say "Norman Walsh", for example—by specifying a startkey of ["author/364"], and an endkey of ["author/364",{}].

As you may have noticed, one limitation of using relationship documents is that you can only include data from one side of the relationship in your view's output. When querying for books and related authors, we were able to get book data (the books' titles) but not author data. When querying for author and related books, we were able to get author data (the authors' names), but not book data. However, you'll notice that we emitted the author identifiers (in the first example) and book identifiers (in the second example) within the value column. We could have used these values to make additional requests to the database for the needed data or indicated in our query that we wanted documents included in our result set using the include_docs parameter (since we're emitting JSON objects containing a key of _id with a value of the related document's identifier).

Alternatively, you could duplicate a subset of the related data in the relationship documents. This would allow you to access that data when building your view. For example, you could add the book titles and author names in the book-author relationship documents. You could then emit these as the values, rather than (or in addition to) the document identifiers. However, duplicate data risks becoming inconsistent as CouchDB does not support transactions across document boundaries.

Get even more for your money.

Join the O'Reilly Community, and register the O'Reilly books you own. It's free, and you'll get:

- $4.99 ebook upgrade offer
- 40% upgrade offer on O'Reilly print books
- Membership discounts on books and events
- Free lifetime updates to ebooks and videos
- Multiple ebook formats, DRM FREE
- Participation in the O'Reilly community
- Newsletters
- Account management
- 100% Satisfaction Guarantee

Signing up is easy:

1. **Go to: oreilly.com/go/register**
2. **Create an O'Reilly login.**
3. **Provide your address.**
4. **Register your books.**

Note: English-language books only

To order books online:

oreilly.com/store

For questions about products or an order:

orders@oreilly.com

To sign up to get topic-specific email announcements and/or news about upcoming books, conferences, special offers, and new technologies:

elists@oreilly.com

For technical questions about book content:

booktech@oreilly.com

To submit new book proposals to our editors:

proposals@oreilly.com

O'Reilly books are available in multiple DRM-free ebook formats. For more information:

oreilly.com/ebooks

O'REILLY®

The information you need, when and where you need it.

With Safari Books Online, you can:

Access the contents of thousands of technology and business books

- Quickly search over 7000 books and certification guides
- Download whole books or chapters in PDF format, at no extra cost, to print or read on the go
- Copy and paste code
- Save up to 35% on O'Reilly print books
- **New!** Access mobile-friendly books directly from cell phones and mobile devices

Stay up-to-date on emerging topics before the books are published

- Get on-demand access to evolving manuscripts.
- Interact directly with authors of upcoming books

Explore thousands of hours of video on technology and design topics

- Learn from expert video tutorials
- Watch and replay recorded conference sessions

Spreading the knowledge of innovators   safari.oreilly.com

Ingram Content Group UK Ltd.
Milton Keynes UK
UKHW032253240423
420706UK00009B/142